BORN TO FLY

BORN TO FLY

written by
General Edwin W. Rawlings USAF (RET.)
in collaboration with
Dr. Edwin B. Stone, Ph.D

GREAT WAY PUBLISHING
Minneapolis, Minnesota

Copyright © 1987 by General Edwin W. Rawlings

First Edition

All rights reserved. Except for brief excerpts for review purposes, no part of this book may be reproduced in any form without written permission from the publisher.

GREAT WAY PUBLISHING, MINNEAPOLIS, MN 55426

ISBN 0-9619320-0-7

LIBRARY OF CONGRESS CATALOG CARD NO. 87-82697

Manufactured in the United States of America

Dedicated

to

my many military and civilian
friends, without whose help
and encouragement this book
would not have been possible.

Contents

Dedication V
Table of Contents VII
Foreword I IX
Foreword II XIII
Introduction XV
Acknowledgements XVII

PART I

Chapter I	Born To Fly	1
Chapter II	Wings Sprout	12
Chapter III	In The Sky	23
Chapter IV	A Career Comes Into Focus	35

PART II

Chapter V	At War	44
Chapter VI	More Stars	56
Chapter VII	Air Logistics	67
Chapter VIII	A Military Career Ends	79

PART III

Chapter IX	A General to General Mills	91
Chapter X	Improving Profits	103
Chapter XI	People Power	115
Chapter XII	Enjoying The Fruits	129

PART IV

Chapter XIII	Computer Consortium	140
Chapter XIV	Future Military Management	154
Chapter XV	Better Business	166
Chapter XVI	Into The Future	176

Foreword I

The reader will find this autobiography of retired Air Force General Edwin W. Rawlings a real-life American success story about a man with great courage, vision and determination. As General Rawlings describes it: "I didn't write the script, but I played my part to the hilt" and he did!

As a young officer, I was privileged to serve as a Major on General Rawlings' staff when he was the Commanding General of the Air Force's Air Materiel Command. Later, when I retired from the Air Force and he from a second, illustrious career as Chairman of the Board of the General Mills Corporation, we became close friends and frequent correspondents.

In my role as Executive Director of the Air Force Association, and its Aerospace Education Foundation, I witnessed General Rawlings' intense interest in inspiring the nation's young people and challenging them to emulate — and top — his own personal achievements. The large Minneapolis chapter of the Air Force Association honored him by adopting his name; he responded by leading this chapter and his community in major civic and aerospace educational activities. All the while he was generously honoring friends, families and countless young men and women with educational fellowships and grants in their names.

The anecdotal chapters of his autobiography are instructive for

Born To Fly

both young and old; he has done all generations a great service by sharing personal vignettes that combine to present testament to his genius and inspiration for his readers. We can share with him his vigorous childhood experiences, his athletic endeavors, his early business acumen as a "pots and pans" salesman — attributes that launched him on the road to becoming a wartime logistics czar. They relate to his selection to attend Harvard Business School and, later, to his unique achievements as the first Comptroller of the new United States Air Force, Finally, culminating his Air Force career as Commander of the huge Air Materiel Command, responsible for supplying and supporting the worldwide requirements of the entire Air Force, and charting the course of his second career in the top executive positions of the General Mills Corporation.

General Rawlings provides the reader a rare insight into the strong leadership of the embryonic post-World War II Air Force by its first Secretary, Stuart Symington. He describes his request to Secretary Symington in 1947 for early (20 year) retirement to accept an offer to join G. H. Walker's New York investment banking firm. Symington denied the request in a most unusual manner by placing an immediate telephone call to Mr. Walker (with General Rawlings listening) and told him: "Herby, Ed Rawlings will not be accepting that job with you. I have just made him the first Comptroller of the Air Force!"

In this new Air Force Comptroller capacity, General Rawlings relates an episode (one that has become legend in the Air Force circles, I might add) in which he ingeniously arranged to transfer $100,000 from the Air Force budgetary line item "Industrial Planning" to the Census Bureau budget accounts, in exchange for one of two of the Census Bureau's newly-conceived and constructed pieces of Sperry calculating equipment called "computers!" It was to be the very first computer used in the Department of Defense.

Retiring from the Air Force in 1959, as the four-star Commander of Air Materiel Command, General Rawlings determined never to abandon the Air Force that had given him such remarkable opportunities. He writes, "I resolved to remain in the Air Force in spirit. There were too many close ties...there were people I would never forget...institutions that I had helped to sire that I would never disown." One of these was the Air Force Academy where he has been

Rawlings

a tireless supporter of philanthropic programs and activities. His work with the Academy's Foundation, and its related Falcon Foundation, has firmly established General Rawlings' place in its history. He has made frequent personal contributions and encouraged countless others to provide scholarships at specialized preparatory schools to enable highly qualified young men and women to gain admission to the Academy. Within the many Air Force related civic and community programs throughout the Nation, his involvement and his tireless participation have firmly established him as one of the principal Senior Statesmen of our service.

His "second career" is equally illustrious! Joining General Mills in 1959, as Financial Vice President, General Rawlings maintained the verve and dynamism that had marked his Air Force career. He became deeply immersed in all aspects of General Mills' vast production and marketing activities; his interests ranging far beyond the traditional financial activities. He gave this corporation the same total commitment and loyalty he had given the Air Force, turning down an early offer of the Presidency of TWA. It was no surprise that, within two years, he was made the President of General Mills.

As President of this giant food processing corporation, he took an unprecedented step, completely out of character for giant milling corporations, and sold the traditional — but unprofitable — flour milling business. Many in the business and the community considered this unheard-of-divestiture to be tantamount to sacrilege; but, General Rawlings saw his corporation's gross revenues increase ten-fold and its profits increase forty times over! Another tribute to the prescience of this unusual man.

The personal side of his life is portrayed with tenderness and candor; from his childhood romance with his sweetheart, Betty, to his romantic meeting and marriage in Hawaii to his beloved "Pete" — mother of his four children and wife of more than five decades. He will capture the attention of all sportsmen readers with numerous accounts of his lifetime "love affair" with hunting and fishing; pursued with a fervor that marks General Rawlings as a world-class sportsman. Then there was the legendary (and imaginary) romance with "Betty Crocker," of General Mills' kitchen, whose name adorns their many bakery products and whose culinary fame is worldwide. General Rawlings describes "Betty Crocker" as the illusory mistress of all

Born To Fly

General Mills employees — a household word synonymous with quality baking and foolproof recipes. He gives "Betty Crocker" credit for a large portion of General Mills' success and professes undying love and admiration.

His storybook romances do not end here, however. In the final portions of his book, General Rawlings concludes his romantic adventures with a recounting of his later-life meeting with Kathy Fradkin during one of his many extended stays in Honolulu — a companionship that blossomed into a mature romance. At age 82, he married Kathy in the fall of 1986 in a memorable ceremony in the Chapel of the Air Force Academy, attended by General and Mrs. Curtis E. LeMay as best man and matron of honor. The chapel was filled to overflowing with families, friends and well wishers — including a reunion of his class at Harvard Business School, Trustees of the Falcon Foundation and colleagues of Ed and Kathy's from throughout their illustrious lives. For a finale to these poignant weekend activities, there was a reception at the fabulous Broadmoor, a classic (and successful) Air Force-Navy football game and a biting, early fall Colorado snowstorm! Then, turning to his other love, General Rawlings went fishing.

General Rawlings is a convert to the "case study" teaching method in use by his alma mater, the Harvard Business School. His book stands as a major contribution to the effectiveness of that teaching method for it is a detailed "case study" of the successful, real-life story of one of our nation's best known and most respected military/civilian leaders of the 20th century.

I am privileged to call Ed Rawlings my friend. This book explains why!

                      Russell E. Dougherty, General, USAF (Retired)

June 1987

Foreword II

My greatest privilege in life was to serve under General Rawlings as an officer, at Wright Field.

In my opinion he was the greatest financial officer in the Air Corps and later in the Air Force. He was a brilliant administrator and had the complete respect of all the officers that ever served with him.

Upon his retirement, he became President of General Mills, one of the largest corporations in this country and did a magnificent job in building that corporation to its present greatness.

It is my greatest privilege to be able to say so much about such a wonderful friend and able man. He is understandably proud of his successful and varied lifetime accomplishments. His record in Air Force Administration and Business Administration is unequaled...and in *"Born To Fly,"* he tells his story very well and ever so interestingly. Read it — and enjoy!

June 1987

W. Thayer Tutt,
Chairman El Pomar Foundation
Chairman Air Force Academy Foundation
Chairman Broadmoor Hotel

Introduction

Every person's life is a learning experience, for himself and for others. What a loss that most take it to the grave with them. Except for the people they brushed shoulders with, all they leave to posterity are the words of their epitaph. Even their closest family members and peers soon file that life's lessons under memories.

My learning experience has been too exciting to come by and too valuable to be squandered. It contains lessons for young people with stars in their eyes on how to reach those very stars.

It contains lessons to enable our country's officials to recognize what might be fatal weaknesses and to correct them and transform them into strengths.

It contains lessons for business people to turn losses into profit and profit into greater profit.

It contains lessons for politicians to become statesmen and statesmen to become world leaders.

I take no credit for curriculum. I did not write the script. But I played my part to the hilt. My part was as a student in the classroom of life. If money in a bank, happiness in a day, and medals, honors, and awards on a wall are any kind of a report card, I was an A student.

I believe this qualifies me to teach. That is, to teach the lesson I know best: my life.

No, I did not write the script for that life. But I write the book now, the book that portrays it. I apologize to the reader for omitting the last chapters. They will probably be the best. But come live my life with me now on the pages ahead and you will have a ball. I did.

Colorado *General Edwin Rawlings*
August, 1987 *USAF (Retired)*

Acknowledgements

To **Stuart Symington** — had he not kept me in the Air Force and made me its first Comptroller this book might not have been written.

To **Gene Zuckert** — who gave me unending support in building the Air Force Comptroller organization.

To **Charlie Bell** — whose faith in me made it possible to come to General Mills and then rise through the ranks to become Chairman of the Board and C.E.O.

To **General Eaker** — whose recommendation to Secretary Symington caused me to turn down my request for early retirement.

To **Mort Wilner** — who came to my rescue a number of times, both in the Air Force and in business life.

To **Thayer Tutt** — the best Personnel man I have ever known. He had the ability to get the right man for the right spot and, contrarily, he knew, rather than try to fit a square peg into a round hole, how to get him out of the way without any fuss.

To **Sergeant Atkins** — whose excellent driving always got me to my appointments on time.

PART I

Chapter 1

Born To Fly

"**H**ave you seen Edwin?" Ella Mae Rawlings called to her husband. It was time for Sunday lunch and her four year-old son was nowhere to be seen. This was nothing unusual, so Frank Rawlings gave an unconcerned "No, dear," and went on reading.

"Edwin, Edwin!" Ella Mae Rawlings was now shouting out the window, first on one side of the building, then on the other, then out the door at the front of the stairway between the grocery and hardware store. Her voice became more shrill as her concern mounted.

Frank Rawlings put down the Farmer's Almanac and said he would go look. As he passed her on the stairs, he patted her on the cheek. "Don't worry, he's probably playing in the shed."

"That boy has a way of disappearing from the face of the earth and re-appearing, just as mysteriously," she said, wiping her hands on her lace-trimmed apron. "Find him and get him back here before lunch spoils."

"Edwin! Edwin!" I don't know how long my father had been calling me when I heard his voice. It was persistent, but not angry. I knew he was just reassuring himself that I was all right. I was fine. But I was in a place where I had lost track of time.

I was airborne, supported by a wooden platform, 50 feet high in the sky. A huge windmill was slowly turning, its blades propelling

Born To Fly

me through space. I looked down at my father. He was putting his hands on the sides of his mouth as he called, "Edwin!"

"I'm up here," I shouted, cupping my hands as he did. He looked up and said something about God. But I was nowhere near that high. I sensed he wanted me to come down, so I got down on my fours and put one foot over the side, searching for the first rung of that funny stairway.

"Careful!" I heard him say. But there was nothing to it. I felt quite at home up there. It was fun going up and fun coming down.

He met me halfway. Two hands grasped me around the waist, and I never reached the ground as he hugged me to his chest. Upstairs, two arms took me from his and I got another hug. I don't remember the walloping I got. I only remember the hugs.

Looking back now, I recognize this as the reward method for behavioral training. Were my parents inadvertantly reinforcing my innate desire to fly? I accepted their concern for the flimsy ladder leading to the windmill. That became off-limits. But trees were still my stairways to the stars. The only problem with trees was that they clung to you. You could not enjoy the wind in your face and have the bird's feeling of flying. But I took care of that.

I found a heavy rope and tied one end to a high limb of a cottonwood tree. To the other end I tied a gunny sack filled with straw. I arranged to be able to climb to the roof of a shed a few feet away and hoist up the gunny sack. Grabbing onto the sack, I could kick off from the shed roof and go flying through the air on my "wings." When this unique swing (which I named 'Billy') finally came to rest. I was safely on the ground. Twenty years later when I made my first solo flight in a real biplane, landing was nowhere as easy as it was on my swing.

My neighborhood friends in Tracy, Minnesota, would watch me enviously and beg for a chance. I must admit I was pretty selfish about lending out my "plane." When somebody else used it, I had to just stand by and watch. But one day when one of my friends was swooping to and fro and I was watching from the shed roof, I called to him, "Hang on, I'm coming, too." On his next swing to the shed, I jumped, grabbing the rope, the sack, and him. Now there were two of us flying through the air together.

Then there were three. And occasionally four. A crew of young boys, and girls, flying through the air together. I never got a 'don't' from my parents, just an occasional 'be careful.' Their authority was not a problem. Since it was my rope, my sack, and my invention, I had special rights over my friends. I began to feel what it was like to be on the other end of authority.

Looking back today, nearly eighty years later, I wonder if my four stars took seed in that gunny sack.

* * * *

My forefathers were all dirt farmers. In those days, that was the hallmark of respectability. Despite being poor, they ate and they raised children, and they survived.

When, as an interested adult, I attempted to trace the Rawlings lineage, I went from England to Maryland to Kentucky and reached a deadend in Indiana. There the courthouse which contained all of the pertinent records had shortly before burned to the ground.

This I do know. Grandfather Rawlings took a free claim a few miles west of Walnut Grove, Minnesota. That free claim deed was signed by President Arthur and now graces the wall of his great-grandson, Peter Rawlings, in Catlett, Virginia. Shortly before he took this claim, my grandfather had married Jenny Nelson, one of seven children of William Nelson, who had taken out a free claim six or seven miles north of the Rawlings claim.

William Nelson had arrived with his bride from Sweden in the 1860s. They traveled from Ellis Island by boat up the Hudson, around Niagara Falls, and across Lakes Erie, Huron and Michigan. They traveled by oxcart to St. Anthony Falls, which later became Minneapolis. Walking alongside the oxcart, grandfather Rawlings caught his leg in the spurs and broke it. He walked with a limp for the rest of his life. Being a stonemason, he was soon helping to build the Washburn Crosby Mill, largest in the world at that time.

Some years later, an explosion leveled that mill despite its heavy stone construction. Dust was the cause. We know now how to control dust in a mill, but even a century later, when I was head of General Mills, we remained alert to that peril. In fact, great-grandfather Nelson would have turned over in his grave to know that his great grandson Edwin Rawlings ordered the final closing and dismantling of the

Born To Fly

Washburn Crosby Mill. How did I, a four-star general in the United States Air Force, become head of a company like General Mills? Sometimes I wonder.

I am told that many young Swedes met their wives for the first time at boatside. That is in fact the way my paternal grandparents met.

On my mother's side, grandfather Frazier had served in the Minnesota Volunteers and fought in the Battle of Gettysburg. His brother was reputed to have been the youngest man in the Union Army. Grandfather Frazier and his wife had five boys and two girls, one of these was my mother. Her brother Jim was my favorite uncle. He gave me rides on his motorcycle, taught me to shoot ducks — in short, he showed me how to be a man.

As they lived only a few miles apart, it was inevitable that my father and mother would meet. After they were married, my father went into the hardware business with one of his uncles. They did well until a series of rainy, wet springs kept farmers from planting crops in Minnesota's short growing season. As a result, the farmers could not pay their bills, and the store went bankrupt. My dad went back to farming and managed to eke out a living.

I attended grade school, then high school, in Tracy, Minnesota. My grades were fair, but nothing to brag about. Being rather tall for my age, and sturdy, I favored sports and the outdoors. Lauren Donaldson, a boy my age whom we called Pete, was my best friend. We were inseparable. He was close to his sister, Rosemund, whom we called Jackie. I was close to my sister Florence, two years my junior. The four of us were always together.

Except there were times when Pete and I would ditch the girls and take off on our bikes.

We had to walk more than a mile to school through some pretty rough woods. There were bears in the area as well as fox and wolves. I seemed to be more tense on these walks than my sister, Florence, two years my junior. By then, I had a much younger sister, Marcella.

When I was thirteen, I purchased a Damascus shotgun for $1.50 at a junk shop. It was a double-barreled hammer gun, obsolete even then. I became interested in hunting and was soon a good shot. I should say that the gun was a good shot, because after I replaced it with a more modern gun years later, it took me a while to become once again as proficient.

Pete and I would pedal our bikes ten miles south to Bloody Lake. According to local residents, it got its name from the blood of early settlers massacred by the Indians in the 1860s. Sometimes, we would bring fishing rods, other times guns, but always camping equipment and rations. We would pitch camp, start a fire, catch a few bullheads, and cook them over the coals, together with a can of beans. What a feast!

Bloody Lake is also where I shot my first duck, a wood duck. It was a beauty. The Damascus did it. The family enjoyed that feast.

Looking back to those early teens, I can think of no event in which I was involved that has any measurable impact on my future. I toed the line at home and in school, but still had the freedom to enjoy my outdoor life. The biggest shock to hit the school was the day the superintendent walked into his office and found a cow there. But I was too serious to have taken part in such a caper.

World War I was under way. Uncles, cousins, and friends were enlisting. How I envied them! One day, still only 13, I made up my mind to fight against the enemy. I would join the Navy. The first step was to have your family doctor give you a physical exam.

After school, I went to Dr. Workman's office and waited for my turn.

"'Edwin Rawlings." The nurse motioned for me to go in.

"Hello, Edwin. How's the family?" And then, without waiting for my reply, Dr. Workman asked, "What's your problem, boy?"

"I need to have you fill out this paper." I gave him the form. He looked at it, then at me, then back at the form.

"Well, this is easy enough." In between listening to my heart and lungs with his stethoscope, thumping my back and chest, and sticking a light in my eyes, ears, and mouth, he carried on a light banter.

"Enlisting in the Navy, are you? What kind of a ship do you think they'll assign you to? Can you swim?"

I answered all of his questions in a serious, intelligent way. He knew I meant business. He also knew I was only 13 years old.

"Well, that's it. You are in good physical shape. You have just passed the Navy physical." He signed the completed form with a flourish. "Good luck." I took the form, thanked him, and marched out

Born To Fly

of his office.

That night I studied the rest of the forms and made my plans to leave in as few days as possible. The next day when I came home from school, my father called to me. He was in the kitchen, sitting at a table with my mother. She was dabbing at her eyes.

"Bumped into Dr. Workman," said my father sternly. "He said you were enlisting in the Navy. Is this true?"

"Yes," I said, "My country needs me."

"But you're only 13," he argued. "The Navy's minimum age is 16."

"I'm big for my age. Some of the 16-year-olds at school are smaller than I am." I was making the best argument I could but surprise was my only hope for victory, and now that the secret was out it seemed my enlistment was off.

"They'd put you in the brig for misrepresenting your age. It's a good thing Dr. Workman didn't report you." My father looked at my mother as if to say, "I've talked to him. Now you talk to him."

She tried to smile, but tears were still in her voice. "We need you here, Edwin. Those who stay behind are needed too. Your father needs to work to feed us. You need to work to buy the things you want and to help with the cost of your education. There are fewer hands to milk cows and bring in the crops."

I nodded. "I'll help out more, Mom."

"Remember what you just said when the snows come," interjected my father. Mother laughed. She knew how skilled I was at avoiding the snow-shoveling chore. That conversation ended with my "punishment," a reassuring hug, first by mother and then by father. So the Navy lost out. It turned out later to be the Army Air Corps' gain.

It was not long before coming events cast their shadows. World War I was over and a second cousin of mine, an airplane mechanic, teamed up with another cousin who had been a pilot in the U.S. air Service. They bought a Jenny Trainer and began barnstorming that part of the country. Sometimes they had to leave the plane alone in the open and so got me to stay and watch it, I was paid nothing. But the privilege of being with that plane was glory enough.

In 1918, at the age of 14, I started my four years at Tracy High School. As I'd already been playing football for a year, I easily made the team. My assigned position was halfback, which gave me the flexibility I liked. I could run, pass, punt, or drop-kick, and I did all three with equal facility. I was what they called a triple-threat player.

I don't remember any spectacularly long runs as a ball carrier, though I managed to tick off above average gains. It was as a punter that I made my name at Tracy High. I could kick the ball with unerring accuracy to the one spot in enemy territory where nobody could possibly catch it. It was nothing for me to drop-kick the ball through the bars at 50 yards. My kicks were not the classic spirals you see today, but more likely were end over end, giving the ball, on landing, an erratic and unpredictable behavior. I averaged 42 yards, which is tops even today. I could also aim my punts to go out of bounds so close to the opposing team's goal line you could hear the spectators gasp. I was a sharpshooter with my foot, and I still look back at those days with pride.

I was also a sharpshooter with that $1.50 Damascus. Lake Seagull was the best place for bluebills when they were migrating, and I would always bring back the full legal limit. At the Marsh Lake Shooting Preserve there was an annual contest, and the trophy was mine several years in a row. In fact, one year I did better than bring down ten birds with ten shots — I brought down eleven, hitting two birds with one shot!

Physical activity was not seasonal with me. I played basketball, enjoyed track events and swam. I guess you might call swimming seasonal as we had no indoor pools and one can't swim on ice.

Another friend of mine at Tracy was "Fats" Long. His real name was Leon, but his oval shape earned him that moniker from our local Boy Scout Troop. He and I vied for the prestige of being the first one in the water each spring.

We would walk along the railroad track. Fats's father was the railroad yardmaster. When he saw us, he would wave us to go on. That job made him an important person to us kids, but he really was one of Tracy's elite.

Where the tracks ran along the side of a lake, Fats and I would watch for a water hole where the ice had just gone out. There was an unwritten agreement among all of us, children and adults alike, not to go out on untested ice. We knew of past tragedies. Fats and I were not reckless risk-takers.

There was an steep, ten-foot embankment down to the ice. Sud-

Born To Fly

denly, I saw Fats spin around and go down the embankment backwards on all fours. I looked ahead. Sure enough, there was an area of clear water. I went down sideways, trickier but faster. In fact, I had my jacket and shirt off when I reached the water's edge. I practically dove out of my pants into the water, surfacing just in time to see the splash made by Fats' bellywop.

"First in," I gasped, when his head appeared.

"Not by much," he spluttered.

The shock of the ice water was not just that momentary twinge that wears off. It was a continuing agony. What price bravery? We helped each other out. The sun-warmed air, though just in the 60s, felt like an oven.

"I thought I had you," shivered Fats. "How'd you get in so fast?"

"With great difficulty," I replied, my teeth still chattering. Then I cheered him up. "There's always next spring."

Funny how a camaraderie builds when you have experienced some daring feat together. Walking back, Fats and I felt like we were the only two people on earth. Certainly we had licked the world.

It was the same kind of feeling that I would later notice among returning veterans. They stuck together, telling and retelling their personal war stories. I envied them their experiences, for they had tasted life. Of course, there were those no longer around to tell their story. But I dwelt on success. I listened to the horrors of the battles from which they had emerged with awe and respect.

Intercepting a pass and running 40 yards for a winning touchdown was my taste of life. Being the first in the icy waters was my battle tale. And I told it again and again, not in the sense of personal glory, but in the sense of sharing with others my taste of life — milking it for all it was worth.

* * * *

I had taken quite seriously the admonition by my parents that I should be earning money and putting some in the bank for my college education. Yes, I shovelled more snow that winter, but here it was spring and I knew some farmers could use help. In fact, every farmer could use help. But no farmer could afford to pay.

It was not until that summer that one offered real money. His immediate problem was mustard growing in his oats. He would pay me fifteen cents an hour to pluck mustard (clean oats meant a higher price).

I got up earlier and I went to bed later and so managed to fit several hours of work into my high school daily schedule, and more on weekends. In a couple of weeks, I had made five dollars, enough to open a savings account. My father went with me. Now I had a bank book.

"How does it feel?" asked my father.

"It felt better to have the green money in my hand." I replied, fingering the booklet.

"Money in the hand is money spent," cautioned my father, "This way you will have it for the time you really need it."

Years later, as Comptroller for the United States Air Force, those words must have still been echoing inside me.

There was more than money in the satisfaction I got from working. It pleased me to know that the farmer was getting a better price for his cleaner oats. On arriving in the morning before school, I also milked his eight cows for him. Then, on returning after school to pick mustard, I milked those cows again. It was hard work. At first my hands were sore and stiff, but then they became used to the task. Having help with the milking was a boon to the farmer, and he was glad to pay me for the time.

That schoolboy satisfaction, of others benefiting from my work, never left me. It was with me in sports. I wanted to win. But, even more, I wanted my teammates to win. It was with me in future jobs. I went the extra mile. It was with me in the military service. The limits of duty were not my personal limits. It was with me in the world of big business. I would not let myself or the company take some profitable action if it was at the expense of individuals.

It was probably a major causal factor in my rise through the military ranks and in my business position.

It was probably behind every one of the scores and scores of medals, honors, and citations that I received over the years.

Where did it come from? Was I born with it? Did I learn it in school? How did I come to instinctively work for more than selfish gain, but for mutual gain?

The answer is not obvious. I have to guess at it. But I would

Born To Fly

suspect my parents' ways are at the root of it. Theirs was not the way of punishment, theirs was the way of reward. They saw that I benefitted by their parental work. Their direction to their children was not just to make life easier and more pleasant for themselves, but to make life easier and more pleasant for the children, too.

Now, at the age of 83, I still have that trait. I hope to prove it to you in this book. If you, the reader, get more benefit and more enjoyment from this book than you bargained for, write me in care of the publisher.

Those awards started when I graduated from Tracy High School. The happiest part of receiving the Dr. Workman Award as Tracy's outstanding student-athlete was to have my family present in the audience to share in the event.

Then along came an even more important award. The summer of my high school graduation, with college financially out of the question, I worked for the owner of Dan Campbell's Resort. My job was to paint the wooden boats and mend bathing suits, and to rent them to vacationers.

It was a boring job, except for the day I opened the door to the hut where I kept the suits and there stood a naked lady. She thought it was a bathhouse. I don't remember what I did, but I do remember I was shocked.

One day when I had a few minutes to myself, I was out kicking a football on the resort grounds. An old Model T Ford pulled up and two young men got out.

"Are you Edwin Rawlings?" called one of them, I picked up the football and approached them.

"Yes, I'm Edwin Rawlings. What is it you want?"

"We're recruiters from Hamline University. This is Bill Kerfort and I'm Glen Krueger." I shook hands with both of them.

"How did you know I was here?" I was puzzled.

"We were over at Tracy High School. They told us about you and said you worked here part time. So we gave it a try." Krueger explained.

I was still puzzled. "But I can't go to college. I don't have the money. Maybe someday."

"Of course we'd like you to pay your tuition like everybody else, but there is another way." Krueger looked at Kerfoot. Kerfoot nodded, Krueger continued, "We can offer you a football scholarship."

I was dumbfounded, but still leery. "Are you authorized to do that?" I certainly hoped they were, because painting boats and mending bathing suits was not on course for me. My heart began to pound with excitement.

Kerfoot pulled out some papers. "My father is president of Hamline and these are application forms for four-year athletic scholarships."

"I have to think it over."

"Don't take too long, you'll miss out," said Krueger. Kerfoot started to put the papers back.

"I've thought it over. The answer is yes," I said, forcing a chuckle. They both laughed and shook hands with me.

"Don't you need a demonstration?" I offered, slapping the pigskin.

"We've seen your record. We didn't even take as long as you to decide. Fill out your name and address. Read the fine print and sign here."

I filled it out and signed. But I couldn't read the fine print. Sometimes, under emotional circumstances, the eyes can't focus on something that small.

Chapter II

Wings Sprout

In early September of 1923, I boarded a Chicago and Northwestern train, bound for St. Paul. In my wallet I had $100, a gift from my father. I was now on my own.

Arriving in mid-afternoon, I located a fleabag hotel and checked in for the night. The next morning I was met by a chap I knew from Tracy, Vic Westman. He took me over to the Phi Delta Theta fraternity and introduced me to many of his fraternity brothers. They rushed me. I joined and went through the initiation. It was called "hell week," but I made light of it. However, my four years in Hamline were over I had made lifelong friends in the Phi Delta House.

But I could not afford to live there. Instead, I found a house near the campus where I got a room free for shoveling snow from the walks, carrying in wood, and doing other odd jobs. I soon learned the ropes on campus, thanks to my fraternity brothers, and was able to arrange additional income for food, clothes, and fun by shoveling, delivering newspapers, and mowing grass.

Fellow student Walter Kolby and I would board a streetcar daily and ride to Midway YMCA where we washed dishes in return for our noon meal. So it was that the social and financial pieces of my college life quickly fell into place; then I was ready for studies and sports, not necessarily in that order.

Football training started before school opened. I made the team.

Later that year, I made the basketball team, then the track team. I was not only earning my scholarship, but giving Hamline University a bigger measure than they had bargained for.

On the gridiron, my kicking got better, averaging 42½ yards. I was the passing halfback and did reasonably well at that, but my foot became better known.

Now, about my studies. Perhaps the less said the better. I was enrolled in a bachelor of arts program, the first year devoted to basic required courses. I ran a C average.

Considering that I was involved in several jobs and in several athletic programs, I did not think that too bad then. My main objective was to help Hamline win games and to do well at track meets — and to graduate with a degree.

During my first Christmas vacation at Hamline, I was able to get a temporary job as a mail handler, helping with the holiday rush of mail aboard the Great Northern line from St. Paul to Winnipeg, Canada.

On one of those trips I was able to purchase a good wool suit for under $100. It was a great buy and I needed such a suit. Back at college after vacation, I received a call to come to the Dean's office. I was told that Postal Inspectors wanted to talk to me.

My heart was in my mouth. What could I have done wrong? Was it the suit I had brought back from Canada? No, I knew Americans were allowed $100 value duty-free. Were there mail bags missing?

when I entered the Dean's office, two postal inspectors started to question me in an accusing tone about a vulgar letter that somebody received which had been traced to my typewriter.

"We know you wrote it," said No. 1.

"We have you dead to rights." echoed No. 2.

"Typewriter type doesn't lie." They insisted.

My head was swimming as they held this vulgar letter up for me to read and a sample of typing they made on my typewriter.

"I never saw that letter before in my life." I insisted.

"You lie." "You lie." No. 2 echoed No. 1.

"But typewriters don't lie. You said so yourself."

"What are you getting at?" asked No. 1 impatiently.

I knew enough about the use of typewriters to know that everybody's touch is different and reveals itself by a different darkness.

Wings Sprout

People also made their own brand of misspellings and typographical errors.

"Get my typewriter. Read the letter to me and let me type it. Then you be the judge."

They agreed, and when it was all over it did not take them long to admit that I did not write that dirty letter. What a relief!

The culprit was later identified. He was a student who had recently been penalized by the Student Cuncil for cribbing. He had then crawled over the transom to get to my typewriter. He was expelled.

That was probably my longest day at Hamline.

When you are busy every day studying, working, competing, the days go by fast. Before you know it, a year has passed and then two and three.

A second cousin, Lester Mondale, was two years ahead of me at Hamline. He is the half brother of Fritz Mondale, who later became Vice President of the United States. Lester worked as a stringer for the St. Paul Pioneer Press, feeding them Hamline University news.

When Lester graduated, he introduced me to the editor of the paper and I became their Hamline stringer. This was a great help to me financially. Now I had no trouble making ends meet and could even up the standard of my clothing a few points. It also meant shoveling less snow.

About a year later I saw an article in the paper about a Spanish Count named Gene Delapana. He was building a log cabin hideaway on an island in Woman Lake near Hackensack, Minnesota.

"There could be a good picture story there, Mr. Dunlop," I suggested to the editor. He gave me a camera and $50 for expenses.

He wished me good luck with the story and I embarked on my first full-fledged newspaper feature. I could write straight news, but this required a fictional style, so I got a fraternity brother, George Peterson, who was editor of the Hamline University newspaper, to join me on the project.

We headed off in an old Model T Ford. We had no idea where to find Count Delapana, so we drove around the lake looking for some clue.

"Let's ask somebody," I suggested.

"But whom?" George replied. There was not even a horse in sight.

"There," I said suddenly, spotting a fine looking young woman sitting on a porch with a young baby in her arms. "I'll ask her."

Approaching the stairs, I called up to her, "Do you know where we can find Count Delapana?"

"He's my husband," she replied.

Following her directions, we soon came upon the cabin. Delapana was no more a Spanish Count than was I, but, seeing two young college boys trying to make a buck, he cooperated. I took pictures of the woodsman building the cabin, and George interviewed Delapana to get material for the story.

It wound up with a full three-quarters of a page in the Sunday edition. This not only paid off well, but also had some happy repercussions. We became good friends of the Delapanas and were invited to tour their luxurious home at 510 Groveland, Minneapolis. As a result of that Sunday feature, Editor Dunlop became more approachable. In fact, it was not long before I approached him for a favor that would be the turning point of my life.

* * *

The big event of the Minnesota winter is the St. Paul Winter Carnival. I saved enough money to go. It was a magnificent affair, with ice palaces, snow sculptures, and an eye-catching parade. Remember, I was a small-town lad and this was before television. I did not know what a parade float was or what a brass band sounded like. I was absolutely awestruck.

I forgot about the cold in which I was shivering and was hypnotized by the spectacle of float after float and band after band. When finally the Grand Marshal moved into view, it was as if I was witnessing the second coming of Jesus. Watching in rapt silence, little did I know that years later I would *be* the Grand Marshal of that same parade, invited by the State of Minnesota.

Hunting continued to be my favorite recreation, and Minnesota was a great place to hunt. I say that even today, after having hunted in a score of other states and many foreign countries. Duck and pheasants were our most likely game, but I hankered to hunt deer. Occasionally we would spot a deer on the outskirts of St. Paul, but never when a gun was handy.

Wings Sprout

One day a fraternity brother and I headed to Woman Lake to hunt deer. We had come across plenty of deer tracks, but no deer. I suggested we ask a friend of mine down the road for some tips.

Bill agreed. When we knocked on the door, my friend emerged. We asked him where the deer were.

"All around," He replied.

"We haven't seen any," chimed in Bill.

"I'll tell you what to do," he said, hitting his pipe on the railing to empty it. I expected next a lesson in the local topography and habits of the deer. Instead, he said, "buy a bottle of moonshine from the fellow in the general store, then give it to old Joe who lives two shacks away."

It sounded like a treasure hunt with more clues to go, but we followed his instructions. Old Joe took the bottle from us like he was expecting it, opened it and took a long swig. Then he pointed to the top of a hill about a quarter mile away. "Watch the brush halfway up," he said, his wizened face showing no sign of any practical joke.

To our amazement, we flushed a deer from the underbrush, just as he said. I aimed and fired. The deer dropped. We had our animal. Looking it over, we found two bullet holes. This would be hard to explain to the boys at the fraternity house. We dragged the deer back to the road, draped it over a front fender, and cooked up a story of how we both shot at it from different directions. We all enjoyed venison for a week.

We hunted girls, too. But being what you might call a football hero and also an excellent dancer, I was really the hunted. When I was in my junior year, I dated one girl who stood out from all the others. We had many good times together. We largely gave up other dates and went steady all that year and the next. I felt eventually we would be married. I will refer to her as Betty, for as you will see later it would be indiscreet of me to identify her.

I was in Economics Class in my Senior year at Hamline and spotted an announcement of a fellowship being offered by Tufts College in Boston. I had always been interested in Business Education so made application. However, a classmate also applied and he was a musician as well as a student. I was a B student but only a broken-down football player.

When the results came in Larry Chidester received the Fellowship. Ten years later, when the Air Corps sent me to Harvard, one of the first persons I met was Larry Chidester who was still at Tufts, but teaching. I felt pretty good being in the Air Corps I loved rather than teaching at Tufts. By coincidence, ten years later Tufts presented me with an honorary degree in Business Administration.

A fraternity brother, Doc Mesker, had become a commercial pilot. One day he offered me a ride. I gave a whoop of joy as my answer. At the airfield, he pointed out the plane, a Standard. He logged out and helped me climb into the cockpit seat just behind him. In a minute we were taxiing to the strip. I looked over the side at the turf. What would happen to it as we took off? Would it recede slowly, rapidly, totally?

Doc gunned the motor and now the ground was rushing past. It became a blur. Then, suddenly, the ground tilted, and at the same moment my stomach dropped into my knees. I stopped looking down and looked at Doc. That centered my equilibrium. From that moment on, I could look around, down, and up. Comfortably I did all three. I was exhilarated by the experience. It was a hundred times better than that gunny sack full of straw.

When we landed, Doc climbed out and extended a helping hand. I refused,

"My turn to take her up," I announced.

He laughed. "Some day," he said, his extended arm insisting. I accepted his hand reluctantly, climbed out with his help, and hung on to his hand, shaking it vigorously.

"Thank you, Doc. It was a great ride."

Lindbergh had made his historic solo nonstop flight to Paris the spring of my graduation. Most red-blooded young men were inspired by him to want a flying career. Including me.

Instead, upon graduating I accepted a position at Dayton's, a Minneapolis department store. I had a B.A. degree with a major in economics. I needed a job and did not have much of a choice. I was told by the personnel man that the top man, Mr. Paul Jelense, needed an assistant and that I was being trained for the position. Where was my training to start? As sales clerk in the housewares department.

All those years of college study just to sell pots and pans! Instinctively I knew that much better was in store for me. So I gave the job all I had. I sold pots and pans like they were going out of style.

Wings Sprout

Then Lindbergh came to town.

There was a parade down Nicollet Avenue in Minneapolis. I had commandeered a good spot on the curb, well ahead of the scheduled time. I looked up. Everybody was hanging out of upper story windows to see their hero go by. He came along, sitting high in the back of a convertible, smiling and waving his hand. The crowd roared and waved back. I thought he looked right at me. He didn't seem any older than I was.

Suddenly, a louder roar eclipsed the crowd. I looked up. Three P-1 fighters zoomed by in tight formation. I gasped as they broke formation and put on a simulated dog fight. They did wing-overs, tailspins, and ear-splitting dives. It was the greatest spectacle I had ever seen. I learned later they came from Selfridge Field to honor Lindbergh.

It lasted only a few minutes in the air over Minneapolis, but it kept right on in my mind. I played it over and over, and, each time I played it back, it said the same thing to me:

"Fly, Edwin, fly!"

Now, every moment I had free I looked into the various approaches to a flying career. One of them seemed right. There was an Air Corps Reserve Unit in Minneapolis, organized by a group of World War I flyers who wanted to keep their "hand on." I joined up and attended monthly meetings. No flying yet, but serious study into the ground operations, maintenance, and supply problems associated with a military flying unit.

My main activities became the Dayton's job, dating Betty, and going to those reserve meetings. Marriage to Betty seemed closer and closer. We were very happy together and we discussed marriage as if it were only a matter of time and money. She had a job as a teacher. That would help.

At one of the reserve meetings, a chap from Dayton's sat next to me and mentioned that he was taking a Flying Cadet examination the following week. My ears perked up.

"What's that lead to?" I asked.

"If I pass, I can go to flying school for a year. I get $75 a month plus room and board. If I make the grade there, I become a pilot and automatically get a Second Lieutenant commission in the Air Corps Reserve."

It was like a voice from Heaven ordering me what to do. I felt goose bumps up and down my spine. Since it was probably a competitive exam, I did not want to show my excitement. Instead, feigning naive curiosity, I asked, "What does one have to do to take the exam?"

"Forget it," he replied, "you have to get a letter of authorization from the War Department."

I did not forget it. I thought of Mr. Dunlop of the St. Paul Pioneer Press. Remember, I said I was to ask him a favor that would change my life. I phoned him and told him my problem.

"Hey, Edwin," he replied, "I've a friend who is a Congressman. He happens to serve on the House Armed Services Committee. Maybe he can help."

The following week I had telegraphic authority to take the Flying Cadet examination! It came just in time. When I reported to the St. Paul Armory, there were 100 eager young men waiting. They were not all from Minnesota. Many were from Wisconsin, Iowa, and the Dakotas.

The tests lasted two days. Only four made the grade. I was one. The class would not start at March Field, California, until the first of March and this was October. There were only a limited number of openings. We would be notified soon.

The notification came. Only one of the four could be admitted, I was the one.

I was elated. It was a triple victory. I would serve my country. I would learn to fly. I would get married. I went to Betty's house with the good news.

I took both her hands in mine, facing her and looking into her eyes, so she could see the excitement in mine.

"Betty, we can set the date!"

She broke into a look of ecstatic joy. "You've gotten a promotion!"

I shook my head. "No, better than that. Your future husband will never have to sell pots and pans again. I've won an appointment to flying school. I'll leave soon for March Field in California."

She pulled her hands away from me and spun around, turning her back. She put both hands up to her face. I was confused. Were those tears of joy? Or. . .

Wings Sprout

"Betty?" I walked around but she kept turning and hiding her face from me. "When shall we set the date for?"

Finally, she faced me. There were no tears, only anger in her eyes. "Edwin, you say you love me and want to marry me. Then you give up a good steady job at Dayton's with opportunities for advancement to become just a 'fly-boy.'

Now my temper rose. "Fly-boy! You mean a Second Lieutenant in the U.S. Army Air Corps Reserves. Is that a fly-boy? Is our country defended by fly-boys?"

She cooled off as I heated up. "I love you, Edwin. But my idea of a secure, happy life does not include Army flying and drum-beating."

The argument continued for nearly an hour. We both lost. She lost the man she loved. I lost the girl I loved. There were a few phone calls after that, each unsuccessfully trying to convince the other. What I did not know was — I had really won. But that realization came at a time when I could not take advantage of the victory.

On February 22, 1929, I boarded the Union Pacific in Minneapolis, bound for California. It was 23 degrees below zero. I could not see the few friends who had come to see me off because the car windows were frosted over. Anyhow, Betty was not one of them. As the doors closed and the train got under way, frost from each passenger's breath filled the air, but then the car warmed up and I began to feel better.

The first few hours of that trip were a sudden respite from the hectic days of preparation that went before. It gave me time to think. Here I was a military man, dedicating the next years of my life to serving my country. Was that what I really wanted to do? If not, I could get off at the next stop.

It was indeed what I wanted to do. My regard for my country was unbounded. My desire to fly was irrepressible. Flying for my country was my destiny. I felt it. I knew it. Here I was taking off for that career on Washington's Birthday. It was like God saying, "My will be done."

But could I risk my life? Could I be brave when the chips were down? Could I be the fearless, tireless warrior that my superiors would demand of me? Could I fly into flak without flinching? Parachute perilously, maintain my cool under fire, endure hardship, and come up ready for more?

I thought of my prowess with a gun, already proven many times over. I thought of my physical skill on the football field, on the basketball court, and in track. That, too, was undisputable. I remembered the economic hardships which I survived. My firm conclusion: I was well-trained for and capable of the job awaiting me.

I sat back, relaxed, and enjoyed that ride.

Three days later I arrived in Riverside, California. It was mild and sunny. A panel truck was waiting to take me and a few other cadets to March Field.

No barracks were available, so we were assigned to four-man tents. Four cots with a Sibley stove in the center. We had the rest of that day and all of the next to get settled and acquaint ourselves with the facilities available — the latrines, the mess hall, the post exchange. I got to know my tentmates — Ray Knight of Kansas, Carl Feldman, also of Kansas, and Ray Rowe of Illinois.

On the very day of our arrival a Santa Ana wind began to blow, and the temperature dropped. I had never seen such blowing sand. I could hardly breathe. It got into everything, including the food. If you'll pardon the pun: true grit. Nature was testing us, separating the men from the boys. It was so cold we had to take turns stoking the stove to keep warm. We kept our flying suits on and stuffed newspapers in our mattresses.

We were "all ready and accounted for" when the time came for our assignment to training flights. My instructor was Lt. Pinky Griffith. Trained at West Point, he was a sharp officer and an excellent trainer.

First came some ground work, orienting us to the plane we would fly, air rules, and local terrain. Then we flew with our instructor in a plane that had dual controls. Lt. Griffith would take off and have me handle the controls aloft for such basic maneuvers as turning and climbing. But his own hands never left the controls. It all felt so natural to me, I wondered why he never really let go so I could actually be in control. He knew what he was doing; he wanted to make sure I knew what I was doing.

After a few flights with this dual instruction, Lt. Griffith would turn the controls over to me for longer and longer stretches and even for parts of the takeoff and the landing.

Wings Sprout

One day he pulled the plane to the end of the runway, got out of the pilot's seat, and announced, "It's all yours!" After only nine hours of dual control instruction, I was being given the chance to fly the plane solo!

I took off. The plane's wings were like my wings. What a feeling to be in control, flying the blue skies of southern California! I sniffed the air. I could smell the orange blossoms. Following instructions, I made several banks, swung around the airstrip, and came in for my first landing. 'It better be a good one,' I said to myself. It was. Graceful. Smooth. Not so much as a bounce.

I taxied the plane over to where Lt. Griffith was standing. He shook my hand.

"Congratulations, Rawlings," he said, "I am quite pleased with your first solo flight."

I felt like leaping into the air with joy. But I maintained my military dignity. . .at least until I got back to the tent. There I let out a "Wahoo!" that they must have heard in Nevada. I was on my way!

Chapter III

In The Sky

I continued to fly solo every flying day. Lt. Griffith continued to coach me in the basics of primary flying, using not only the PT-1, but also the slightly more advanced PT-3.

In four months we were ready for Basic Training. Now, we were flying World War I DH-4's with 400-horsepower Liberty engines. My instructor was Lt. "Woopy" White.

What a thrill the first time one does a slow roll! My instructor showed me how to keep the nose of the plane on the horizon and stop the roll by applying ailerons. Hanging on by your lap belt upside down, you are fearful it might give way and off you would go into space. But then, there was always your parachute, so there was no point in being afraid.

In another four months we graduated from Basic and were ready for Advanced Training. The Basic instructor who checked me off, approving me for Advanced, was Lt. Nathan Twining. He later became Chief of the Air Force and then Chairman of the Joint Chiefs of Staff.

Advanced training would be at Kelly Field in Texas. I was ready to fly there, but instead we were trucked to Ontario, California, and put on a Santa Fe train headed south.

It was a different train ride than the one I had taken from Minnesota earlier in the year. Then I was riding into the unknown. Now

In The Sky

I was riding into what I knew was to be an exciting future. Surrounding me, instead of the strangers of before, were my buddies who were to be sharing a similar stimulating future. We had a lot to talk about together and the time passed quickly.

Kelly Field was my first exposure to the South. I liked the weather, the Mexican food, and the girls. When I mailed postcards back to my family in Minnesota, spelling out my new address, I included one to Betty. She was out of my system by now, but I wrote her anyway — as a friend.

My assignment was to the Observation Section. It was headed by Captain Pop Gravely. He taught me the ins and out of spotting artillery fire and other facets of aerial observation and reporting. We learned to read maps and operate a radio.

I learned a great deal about the Air Corps at Kelly. Most was part of the training, some I learned on my own. I was interested in the planes I flew, but I was also interested in other planes. What did they have that was different, and why? An important flying maneuver we practiced was the spin. A flyer had to know how to get in and out of a spin to live, so I practiced stalling the plane until it fell off into a spin. The earth became a whirling top. By applying full reverse controls, you could slowly come out of it. Once you mastered it, it was great fun.

When the four months of training were up, there was a full dress graduation ceremony where we were given Pilot's Wings and a Commission as Second Lieutenant in the Army Air Corps. It was just a year after I had left Minneapolis on that frigid morning.

About a month before my stint at Kelly was over, we were given the opportunity to volunteer for assignment to Panama or Hawaii. I chose Hawaii and got it.

Why Hawaii? I had only a vague concept of the Islands. Warm weather. Fine beaches. But what stood out in my picture of Hawaii were beautiful girls in grass skirts!

We were given two weeks leave. I went home to Tracy, proudly wearing my wings and Lieutenant bars. My parents beamed. I bumped into Betty. She seemed impressed, too.

On February 25, 1930, I boarded an army transport ship in San Francisco, *The San Mahiel*. We docked on the morning of March 1st. I was up early, my gear packed, ready to disembark as the island of

Rawlings

Oahu appeared on the horizon. It had a mysterious, beckoning look. An hour later we were sailing into Honolulu harbor and approaching the pier.

It was crowded with people and a band was playing. As ropes were thrown to the pier, I could see girls in grass skirts doing the hula to exotic island music played by the Royal Hawaiian Band.

I was an officer in the Air Corps. A military representative of my country. A pilot. And now in Paradise, too?

I was assigned to the 5th Observation Squadron, Fifth Composite Group, Luke Field on Ford Island just outside of Honolulu. By this time, orientation to a new station was a simple matter for me. I could write the procedures myself.

Orientation to Hawaii — that was another matter. The days went by and added up to weeks, and each day brought new sights, new friends, new experiences. I saw the hula danced; I ate poi (only once); I viewed the island from the Pali; I rode in an outrigger canoe; I surfed; I learned some Hawaiian words like aloha and wahine; I dated some of the latter. I met a beautiful Chinese girl whose name was Winona Love. She was an excellent dancer and a very special girl. We enjoyed dancing under the banyan tree at the Moana Hotel. The stars glimmering in the sky provided a romantic backdrop. Never in my wildest dreams as a 2nd Lieutenant did I imagine that I would have a table every morning right next door at the Royal Hawaiian Hotel. Starting in 1983, and to this day, this table has had a brass and wood plaque bearing the inscription "The 4-Star Breakfast Club — D. Thacker and General E.W. Rawlings." Here, leaders and friends from around the world join me for breakfast.

For now, I commanded the Fifth Photo Section in the Fifth Composite Group. One morning I took an early flight around Molokai before maneuvers, where I spotted a huge whale, at least 100 feet long, on her side nursing her calf. I turned to ready the camera — but it was not there, the only time I have ever flown without my camera. What a missed opportunity!

On May 24, 1930, the combined forces of Luke and Wheeler Fields took off for the Big Island on a practice maneuver. I was in a Loening Amphibian with an inverted engine, capable of smooth-ocean landings and takeoffs, flying escort for the bombers, assisted by my crew chief.

In The Sky

When we were about halfway between Kahoolawe and the Big Island, one of the bombers went into a slow spin. I watched for him to pull out. He did not. Instead, the three white chutes blossomed out behind, a fourth one becoming entangled in the tail and fluttering down with the plane into the ocean.

Before that plane hit the water, I was already on the way down for a water landing. The waves were 30 feet high, the roughest water in Hawaii as the channel is shaped like a funnel and the trades tend to pile the water high. I landed close to the first man to hit the water, but he missed grabbing onto my wing. However, a Navy Martin bomber with high wings and big mounted motors spotted us and was able to land downwind. Now this flying boat was able to rescue all three parachutists.

An inter-island steamer met them en route. The personnel wanted to get aboard but the water was so rough the ship could not come alongside. Then the ship's crew put out a boom with a sugarnet in the end of it. The rescued fliers and the Martin crew crawled onto the sugarnet and were hoisted aboard.

Meanwhile, I was doing all I could to keep my plane afloat. There was great danger of it capsizing in those 30 foot waves. I was using the ailerons as rudders. It was the only way I could keep headed into the wind, which was our only chance. I swallowed a lot of salt spray. Soon I was sick as a dog. And I had once wanted to join the Navy? As I struggled to keep afloat, a plane flew over. I shot a flare pistol. No response. This happened several times.

For nine long hours, my chief and I struggled to keep the plane afloat. It was eight o'clock in the evening when a long boat appeared nearby. It came closer. I could make out a man in uniform and a couple of local men at the oars. It was swept up on a high wave.

"Jump in," yelled the officer.

Being a brand new Lieutenant, I had only one uniform and that was in a small bag on my plane. I could not afford to lose that uniform. I told my chief to go first while I got the small bag. Then I climbed onto the nose of the plane, bag in hand. When the next wave came, I jumped. I missed the boat and went under. When I surfaced, there was my bag. I grabbed it and threw it into the boat.

"Get in!" yelled the Captain, irked by my delay. Then I put my arm over the boat's gunnel and crawled aboard. The officer was the pilot of the Martin bomber who had picked up the others.

"You all right?" he asked me.

"Fine," I sputtered. "How are the others?"

"All safe aboard that steamer."

Now I could see that boat in the darkness. Again, we could not get aboard because of the massive movement of those rough seas. Once again the boom and sugarnet were deployed; we were lifted aboard and plunked down on the deck. The first one I met was my roommate. He was the pilot of the crashed bomber!

It was 8 P.M. and starting to rain. We took shelter inside, and I said a silent prayer of thanks to God that I was saved. The ship headed for Honolulu. We had no radio and were unable to report our position, the loss of planes, or the saving of lives. We would arrive in the morning.

As I rested on a makeshift mattress in the dark, I tried to get a handle on that day. I played it back over and over. Had I done the right thing in risking my plane to save lives? Yes, human life has priority over material. Had I risked my own life in the process? Possibly. But my mission was to escort, and when the mishap occurred I did my escort duty. Military duty has priority over your own safety. I felt satisfied with Lt. Edwin Rawlings. It was as if this had been the first test of personal resiliency. I gave myself a passing grade and fell asleep for a few hours.

At 8 A.M. we pulled into Honolulu harbor. When the news reached Headquarters, there was much rejoicing. They had known nothing of our fate all night long. Our flight surgeon put us on two weeks sick leave so we could get ourselves back into shape.

All I needed was about two hours.

The very next evening I was challenged again. This time I needed a different kind of bravery in order to be a winner.

Luke Field had practically no single men, so my group was quite in demand. We were constantly being invited to luaus and parties. I was assigned to a family-type house which I shared with Lt. Tommy Boyd. One cocktail party was given by an officer and his wife who lived in town. She was the daughter of a prominent local physician, and the whole family was considered upper crust. So when I was invited I readily accepted.

When I walked in the door and shook hands with the hosts,

In The Sky

my eyes fell upon a vision across the room. I will never forget this first sight of her; a beautiful girl wearing a big, picture hat. She was the most exquisite lady I had ever seen.

It took me but a few minutes to maneuver my way to her side and to engineer an introduction. Her name was Muriel Peterson.

"But my friends call me 'Pete,'" she said. "Please call me Pete."

"If that's an invitation to be your friend, I accept." I replied, knowing full well I would start right then to try to upgrade the relationship.

We spent the rest of the evening catching up on each other's lives. Then we kept seeing each other.

I was madly in love with Pete. She was my ideal. Even when I was flying, I thought of her, and that was something rare for me. There was only one thing do do: marry her. After the fourth or fifth date, late that month of May, I proposed.

We were engaged and set the date for two months later, in July, The Petersons sent an engagement announcement to my parents. They notified the newspapers and the news was forwarded to the Minnesota papers. I received a cable from the Quartermaster at Fort Mason, California, asking me if I would authorize transportation to Hawaii for "your fiancee" Betty.

My immediate one word reply was "No." And I forgot about it.

Pete and I were to be married in Central Union Church. It was to be a big wedding. The wedding gown and bridesmaids' dresses were all ordered.

Then Betty arrived in Honolulu. I was notified by the phone that she was waiting for me. I called Pete and told her what had happened. "She must have twisted that Quartermaster's arm," I said. "What will we do?"

"Well, I guess you'll have to go and face her," replied Pete. "You have two women expecting to be your bride. You can't have us both. You'll have to make a choice."

"I choose you, Pete, hands down. I won't face her. Let's get married now."

"You mean today? But..."

"I know, the invitations are printed, the dresses are ordered, the church is reserved, But let's do it, Pete."

"Okay. Let's do it, Ed."

So we did it.

While we rushed to complete our updated wedding plans, a lieutenant friend of mine arranged to keep Betty occupied and out of the way.

Pete called an old family friend, Walter Frear, who was a former judge and governor of the islands and then president of Bishop Trust Company. She asked him if he could marry us at noon the next day. I could see that Pete was disappointed by his answer, so I decided to use my sales ability and took the phone. He said he had a funeral in the morning and a funeral in the afternoon.

"What are you doing in between?" I asked.

"Having lunch between two funerals," he replied.

"How about a fast lunch and a fast wedding at noon?" He agreed.

The funerals Judge Frear said he would be conducting involved one of our intended groomsmen, tragically. Lt. Atterbury, was flying a Loening Amphibian that day and spun in on the side of Luke Field. Both he and his crew chief were killed. Their funerals were set for the next day, the lieutenant at 10 A.M., the sergeant at 2 P.M.

So Pete and I started our wedding day, July 17, with a funeral at Fort Armstrong, Lt. Atterbury's. Then we drove up to Tantalus where Mrs. Frear, her daughter, a granddaughter, and Mrs. Caroline Peterson (Pete's mother) were gathered. Soon Judge Frear arrived.

Pete looked beautiful in white. One would never have guessed how quickly that wedding had been arranged. Every thing, including the flowers, were in perfect taste. Judge Frear performed the ceremony and we were man and wife.

We then returned to Fort Armstrong for a second funeral, the sergeant's. It was a day of agony and ecstasy.

Then off we drove to the other side of the island for our honeymoon. I could not help wondering if Betty might show up and ruin it. But I got a call from my lieutenant friend saying Pete's brother, in charge of Matson Line's passenger service, had bought Betty a ticket — so she was on her way home! Pete and I could now fully enjoy our ecstacy.

It is impossible to look back at an event nearly sixty years later and see it as you did at the time. I know now that I knew I was exquisitely happy. I know now that I knew then I was acquiring a beautiful,

In The Sky

intelligent wife. I know now that I knew then that, with my monogamous nature satisfied, I could devote myself more conscientiously to my Army career.

I know now that I could not possibly have known then how supportive of that career Pete would turn out to be. I could not possibly know then the part she would play in my eventually becoming a four-star general and, later, Chairman of the Board of General Mills. I could not possibly know then that she would bear me four sons, each a star in his own right, or that our marriage would last over half a century.

After our honeymoon Pete and I returned to live in Honolulu where she had a combination apartment and studio. As a Second Lieutenant, I was making $199 a month. I had been given a wire-haired terrier, so we began to raise and sell puppies.

It made us enough money to buy a roadster. I bought it from a man named Kastner. Kastner later became a spy, if he was not one already. Ten years later, he would operate a radio homing device that helped to steer the Japanese to Pearl Harbor.

* * * *

The next few months were spent in routine training. Aerial photography was a basic part of it. In spite of its beautiful blue skies, Hawaii was seldom without clouds, usually over the mountains.

Early one morning I asked Sgt. Stolte to get ready for some aerial shots. It turned out to be a perfectly cloudless day. I climbed the 019 to 10,000 feet over Pearl Harbor.

"Look," I shouted to Sgt. Stolte, pointing in the direction of the Big Island. He nodded excitedly, There, 150 miles away, were the Big Island's two peaks, Mauna Loa and Mauna Kea, in clear view, free of their usual shroud of clouds. The pictures Stolte took received praises and plaudits from all who saw them.

Shortly after that I received a call from Colonel Brant, air officer in charge.

"I showed those Big Island shots to a Mr. Moore of the National Geographic Magazine. He's doing a story on Hawaii and needs some aerial shots. Can you take him?"

I took him the next morning. We shot pineapple and sugar cane fields, sandy beaches, cliffs, gorges, and mountains. A few months later, Moore's story on Hawaii was published.

One of my classmates, Bill Scott, came from a wealthy California family. Knowing he was interested in gliders, his father sent him a do-it-yourself glider kit which probably set him back over $2,000. Several of Bill's friends helped him assemble it, then they helped him take it to the Pali where the air currents were ideal for gliding.

The Pali is also a wet, rainy place, Bill had to wait eight or ten days before conditions were favorable. When the day came, he attached a long tow rope to the nose of the glider and the other end to the back of a car. Scott got aboard, gave the go signal, and was soon airborne.

The glider soared to 800 or 1,000 feet and then, before the eyes of his friends, the glider simply disintegrated, Scott dropping to his death.

Apparently, the wrong type of glue had been used, one that softened because of the moisture. That particular tragedy certainly played a part in instilling in my mind the need for adequate specifications and quality control in military procurement.

* * * *

On September 15 our first son was born. We named him Peter. I was soon given a vacation so Pete, Peter, and I went to the Island of Kauai. Pete knew an ex-Yale man there named Lindsey Fire. He had been a classmate of her brother, Fred. He invited us to stay at his place. We went by boat, the only way in those days.

Soon after our arrival, my urge to hunt surfaced, I vocalized that desire to Lindsey.

"You want to get over to Barking Sands," he said.

"I'd be glad to take you, but I have to work." He told me how to get there.

"How'd it get a name like that?" I asked.

"The sand contains a lot of tiny seashells," he explained. "When you walk on them, they make a noise like a dog barking."

I accepted that with reservation. It sounded like he was playing on my gullibility. "What game is around now?"

"Golden plover," he replied. "When you see some plover, throw

In The Sky

your hat in the air. They'll fly right over you and you'll have a good shot at them."

Now I knew he was pulling my leg. "I'll take you snipe hunting tonight," I told him with a straight face. "You'll hold a pillow case with a flashlight in it. I'll beat the brush and they'll run right into the pillowcase."

Lindsey laughed. "I know that one, Edwin. We pulled it on the frosh at Yale. Believe me, I'm not kidding you."

That day I went to Barking Sands, As I trudged over the sand, it actually barked, Well, maybe the plover story was true, too.

The golden plover is an interesting bird, It raises its young in the Aleutians. This land bird then migrates 2,300 miles over water with its young. They arrive in Hawaii the latter half of August and leave in May. When they arrive, they are skin and bones. When they leave, they are fat as butterballs.

In a few minutes, I saw some plover. Looking around to make sure nobody was watching, I threw my hat into the air. I was flabbergasted. The plover swung around and flew right over me, I aimed, fired several times, and got a few.

I appreciated Lindsey's advice after that. Next, I went hunting for Chinese pheasant. They stayed around the sugarcane. Following instructions, I walked along the irrigation ditches. The cane stood ten to twelve feet on either side. As the pheasants flew over the cane, I shot quickly. The birds dropped into the waterway, the only place in a cane field you could find them.

* * * *

When little Peter was about six months old, I was transferred to Brooks Field, Texas. We boarded, with our car, the same boat I had arrived on, *The San Maheil,* and sailed for San Francisco. It was a rough trip. We were both so seasick that little Peter had foster parents for most of those seven days. A sad note: eighteen Second Lieutenants had made that trip to Hawaii from Brooks Field, Now, only ten had survived to return.

We sailed under the Golden Gate Bridge and into San Francisco Harbor on Easter morning. We headed for Los Angeles — I, Pete, Peter, and our two wire-haired terriers.

Rawlings

In Los Angeles we found the country home of Jack Greaves, a classmate of Pete's at Mills College. Since I did not have to report to Brooks Field for over a month, we decided to spend most of that time in this beautiful spot.

Frank Greaves, Jack's father, took me up to the Owens River and into the nearby mountains to fish for golden trout. We rode horseback, and the sights were magnificent. We dismounted and tied up the horses in a way that permitted them to graze and also drink the cold river water.

The fishing was so great we stayed longer than we intended, throwing each golden trout we caught into a nearby snow bank. It was mid-summer, but at that altitude there was still a lot of the white stuff with which I had become so familiar in Minnesota.

It was getting dark when we gathered up our catch and headed back. Going down a steep mountain trail, on horses that were as unfamiliar with it as was I, turned out to be a harrowing experience. Pete and the others had been ready to call out the forest rangers when we arrived safely. There's nothing tastier than grilled, freshly caught, golden trout. Little Peter agreed.

Our stay over, we loaded the car and headed off for Brooks Field, Texas. It was so hot crossing the Arizona desert that we traveled only at night. During the day we stayed in a motel, covering ourselves with wet sheets to try to stay cool. We used the car's hot radiator to heat Pete's formula.

We finally arrived at Brooks Field where I was assigned to the 12th Observation Squadron of the 12th Group. A Captain Griffith was my Commander. There were no quarters available, so we had to rent a house temporarily. I was soon back in the air, learning more about Observation and Reporting from the oldtimers who had learned it the hard way.

Our house was only a short distance from excellent hunting. I took nearly daily advantage of it, bagging mourning dove and quail, enough to eat these delicacies at any meal we so desired.

One day, Lt. Jimmy Hicks and I went on a reconnaissance mission to Ft. Ringgold, Texas. We took our guns along, so that if time permitted, we could shoot some white winged doves.

We completed our mission. Then we hunted and filled our limit of birds. It was my turn to fly our 019 back to Brooks Field.

In The Sky

We took off. At about 500 feet the motor backfired and quit. Fire came up through the cockpit. It burned the skin off my hand and the flames licked at my face.

I went over the side. Because of the low altitude, I wasted no time in pulling my chute cord. It opened too soon and got caught in the tail of the plane.

I weighed 200 pounds. Fortunately, that was sufficient weight that when I hit the end of the shroud lines, I tore the chute loose from the airplane. I landed safely in the soft silt on the Mexican side of the Rio Grande River.

I looked for Jimmy, and there he came, floating down beside me.

"You okay?" he called.

I shook my head affirmatively. The safe landing momentarily overshadowed the severe burns on my hand and nose. I helped him subdue his chute with my good hand, and he did likewise with mine. We heard yelling from the river.

"Hurry! This way." The sergeant in charge of the airstrip had rowed across the river to get us. He seemed agitated and was waving frantically with his hand. "Hurry!"

We gathered up our chutes and made for the rowboat. Just in time. As we pulled from the shore, a squad of Mexican soldiers ran up with drawn bayonets.

"They don't look very friendly," Jimmy remarked to the sergeant.

"They like locking up our boys," the sergeant replied. "It takes the State Department a week or ten days to get them out. You officers were lucky twice today."

But it was really three times that I was lucky. My damaged chute was examined back at Brooks Field.

"No one could jump in that and live," was the report. The watery silt in the banks of the Rio Grande had saved me.

Chapter IV

A Career Comes into Focus

By this time, you would think that those pots and pans back in Dayton's Department Store in Minnesota had been left far behind. Little did I know that they had been following me along, and would play a vital role in the shaping of both my military and civilian career.

One day my Group commander, Major Lackland, at Brooks Field, called me to his office.

"Rawlings," he said, "You went to Hamline University?"

I nodded, wondering what was coming.

"What did you major in?"

"Economics."

"And later you worked for a department store?"

Again I nodded, with growing misgivings.

"Doing what?" he asked.

I was tempted to say "selling pots and pans," but that might lead to Officers Mess. "I engaged in retail activities in the housewares department."

"Rawlings," he proclaimed with finality, "you are our PX manager. You are the most qualified person here for that specialized job."

And so I became the PX manager. The officer named Rawlings, whose desire to fly and to keep flying had not been dimmed

A Career Comes into Focus

one iota by mishap or close call, was — at least for the time being — grounded.

I must say I put all my heart into running a good store. It was the way I behaved. Whether I liked the job or not, I did my best. I did my best now as a PX manager, especially in the gun and ammunition department. If flying was not to be part of my regular work, at least the thing I enjoyed second most would still be there. Most of the men on the base also were hunters, so the revitalized PX department went over big.

One seldom recognizes the small events in life that become vital influences on future events. I never dreamed the pots and pans would put me in a PX, or that the PX would lead to a more important supply role in Dayton, Ohio, to Harvard Business School, to the first Comptroller of the Air Force, to Chairman of the Board of General Mills, to computerization in higher education, and to who knows what else in the future.

Recognizing these small events that mean so much can certainly give a person a greater feeling of control over his life. But since this is impossible, the best thing to do is ride with events, doing your best all the way. In other words, a general precept might be: say "yes" to life.

Things began to move fast now. Remember, it is in the late thirties. Soon World War II would start in Europe. Then Pearl Harbor and the United States' entry into that war. I do not want to halt this kaleidoscopic account to relate each time I participated in my favorite sport, so indulge me now as I share some of my hunting experiences with you.

So you won't think it is all blowing my horn about my sharpshooter eye, let me start with the time a rancher named Johnson in nearby Kerville, Texas, invited me to go turkey hunting on his ranch. He had a huge spread, and I was able to roam freely over it. I spotted a large oak tree that looked like a good turkey roost. About 30 or 40 feet up a slope from this oak tree was a cedar. If I waited quietly under that tree I would have a good chance when the turkeys arrived.

That was not so easily done. The ground was all shale that made quite a noise when you moved, as I found out when I crawled under the cedar's spreading branches.

Rawlings

It was 4 P.M. I waited in a cramped, motionless position under those branches. And waited, It was 5:30 P.M. and beginning to get dark when the turkeys finally arrived to roost in that oak tree. There were six. Big ones. I tried to raise my gun. I was so tense, both from excitement and from cramping, that I could not hold my gun steady. The barrel went around in circles. I fired. All of the turkeys took off. From 25 feet, sharpshooter Rawlings has missed them all!

Downhearted, I headed off to the house and nearly missed that, too, in the dark. Rancher Johnson tried unsuccessfully to cheer me up. A week later, he cheered me a little with the news that a dead turkey had been found nearby. I had wounded one that died, probably the next day.

We used to fly to Ft. Ringgold and McAllen on the Rio Grande for white-winged doves. It is a beautiful and noble bird. It flies faster and straighter than the mourning dove, so you had to shoot fast and straight to get them, and that's exactly what we did. We also flew to the mouth of the Rio Grande for redheads — great eating. And occasionally we made it to Matagorda Island where we could shoot pintails. They gave us a lot of hunting fun.

Over the years, I have enjoyed hours and hours of pheasant hunting in New York, Ohio, Michigan, Minnesota, and others.

Once we went goose hunting near Ottawa, Canada. Our host, RCAF Air Marshal Campbell, said he would have the seven of us dig individual pits in the pattern of a fishhook. When the birds flew into the hook area, he explained, we would each have a shot. We agreed. He woke us the next morning at four.

We each brought a shovel and started to dig. The ground was frozen stiff. It was like trying to dig concrete. The idea was to dig up enough dirt to hide us from the incoming birds, so we did the best we could. Soon, along came seven geese, with more in the distance. A big gander came over me first as I was at the end of the hook. It was only 25 feet high, an easy shot. I let him have it and he came tumbling down.

Our host, who was clear at the other end of the hook, jumped up and yelled, "I got a goose!" But not only had he not got a goose, nobody else did either, because at least fifty that were on their way in scattered at the sound of his yell. We could have shot him.

Well, I could go on and on about my hunting experiences over

A Career Comes into Focus

the years — bagging ducks by the water holes of North Dakota and by the hot springs of Colorado; trout fishing and duck shooting with my four sons in Idaho; using dogs to flush quail in Georgia. I always found enthusiastic recipients for these birds, besides my family, from hungry friends to Veteran's Hospitals.

But let us progress with my new career, the one with its foundation in pots and pans.

Major Lackland liked the way I ran the Brooks Field, Texas, Post Exchange. Soon after, when he was transferred to Wright Field, Ohio, where he took over the Field Service Section, he asked me to fill a gap there that required business skills.

That week, Pete was told by the doctor that she could have no more babies unless she had an operation. Neither one of us wanted her to have an operation.

We decided to wait until we got to Ohio. We both wanted to have another child. Raising children is not easy, for a parent is faced constantly with illnesses and possible accidents. At Brooks we had a good nurse to take care of Peter. But he was always tugging on her skirt. This once caused her to spill boiling water on him. Luckily there was a doctor next door, but the burns were so severe that he ran a temperature of 105. Pete and I prayed night and day. He recovered with no scars.

When we got to Ohio, we found a chiropractor and Pete started treatments to conceive. In a few months she was pregnant and in December, Charles Frederick (whom we nicknamed Gerry) was born.

The U.S. Army was always inviting officers to improve their education. I kept requesting Harvard, never really expecting something to happen. But it did.

I received orders transferring me to Cambridge, Massachusetts, to attend Harvard Business School. Now that I had it, I did not want it. It had a reputation of being really tough. I was happy with Wright Field. Its more sophisticated material duties were a challenge. Hunting in Ohio was fun. I had a second child on the way. Pete was making good friends, we had a good school lined up for Peter. I decided to ask my Commander to get me relieved.

General Robbins looked at me quizzically. "Did I hear

you correctly, Lieutenant? You want to turn down a chance to go to Harvard?"

"Yes, sir, I enjoy my duties here at Wright Field and would like to continue with them."

He riffled through some papers, then looked up again at me. "Lieutenant Rawlings," he said impatiently, "you have been naming Harvard for years as your preference. Now you have a chance to go. I am not going to get you out of it. Request denied."

We were on our way to Boston.

We arrived in Belmont, a suburb of Boston, on a rainy Sunday afternoon. We pulled up in front of our rented house and got out: Pete and I, Peter and Gerry, and the dogs.

Easterners are cold and unfriendly people, I was always led to believe. The opposite was true. Our van had not arrived yet with our personal belongings. As we waited, the owner of our house drove up with a table, folding chairs, and a hot lunch! Then our next-door neighbor came over and introduced himself. He offered to get anything we needed. Cold people? The warmest.

That week we got Peter started in his first school. I felt for him. A new home, new friends, and now that intimidating day for all youngsters: the first day of school.

The next day, I went through it myself — my first day at Harvard Business School, purported to be the most backbreaking academic experience available. And I had asked for it. Was I some kind of a masochist?

The very first week, they gave us an assignment to write a case analysis over that weekend. Harvard Business School began to live up to its reputation. Besides the civilian student body, there were four officers from other services in the class. We soon got together in a study group to help each other.

I thought it was hard right from the start, but then I began to find out what hard *really* was. That first semester was so tough! There was a hurricane. Sturdy elms and maples were felled. The way I felt I was sorry to see Harvard still standing the next morning. All I kept thinking of was what would have happened if I "chickened out." I even thought of how I might get myself hit by a car without getting killed and retire from school without dishonor. But I realized these kinds of thoughts were dumb, that they were failure-oriented, and

A Career Comes into Focus

it was not like me to be thinking them.

I buckled down to give my studies all the time and effort they required. Pete really helped me. She acted as a secretary, writing down in longhand what I would dictate. We burned a lot of midnight oil.

Once you begin to relate to your teachers, you relate better to the problems they hand you. I developed a liking for Professor Walker in Accounting, Professor Davenport in Statistics, and Professor Smith in Basic Business. They presented the material skillfully. I grasped those subjects well and school got a little easier as time passed.

Harvard is a beautiful school. The Charles River adds an aesthetic touch to both Boston and Cambridge, through which it flows to the sea. Harvard's Baker Library is fabulous. I could find anything I wanted there.

My second year at Harvard, Pete became pregnant again. After our third son, Richard, was born, Pete's mother came from Honolulu to help with the new baby. I was delighted because, as willing as I was to help with these responsibilities, I was nervous about graduation and felt that I really needed to "pour it on" those last few months.

I graduated in June, 1939, with distinction — magna cum laude. Pete and I were overjoyed. Orders soon arrived to return to Wright Field in Dayton.

It was impressive enough having a university degree on my record, showing a major in economics, plus experience in retailing, plus success in post exchange management. But now there was a Masters degree in Business Administration from Harvard. I was assigned on my arrival in Dayton to the Administrative Division of Wright-Patterson Airfield.

For the summer we again rented a house, and in the fall we moved to the Base. The Burnsides lived on one side of us, the Puts on the other. Down the street were the Sessums. In back of us and across an open field were our old friends the Hefleys. In front of us was a golf course. I was not a golfer but I was soon using the course for early morning walks.

Rawlings

Moving from one place to another can be a traumatic experience for the average family, and maybe it happens only once or twice as the children are growing up, if it happens at all. However, for a person in the military, moving is almost like an outing. You take it in your stride. As moving becomes less and less a hardship, what happens is a growth in your ability to adjust, to grasp all details, and to handle the unexpected. It is both a growth factor and an educational experience.

Pete and I were now certainly old hands at it. We had the added advantage of having been stationed here two years ago. We were soon leading a routine life, able to fit into our days the things we enjoyed doing most. I was able to spend more time with the boys than I could while at Harvard. I was also able to hunt moose. And Pete and I were able to go to parties and shows and restaurants.

Yes, you can have a peaceful life in the military.

But this was the late thirties and the sounds of war in Europe were beginning to be heard in Dayton, Ohio. I had completed ten years in the Air Corps and was now a Major. I was completely at home with such matters as budgets, material, supply, and maintenance. So when in October, 1940, President Roosevelt announced a large aircraft build-up, the escalation of my duties represented no problem to me.

Wright Field was not an ordinary base. It was the Air Corps' national headquarters. My office became responsible for obtaining production reports from industry and riding herd on them. I had to make realistic appraisals of aircraft manufacturers' capabilities so that production forecasts could be made that would eventually prove to have been reliable. Monthly reports were made that I knew would be funneled up to the Joint Chiefs of Staffs and would form the basis for critical decisions.

Hitler was now running rampant in Europe. He had enveloped the Low Countries and crossed the Maginot Line into France. American forces were not entering the conflict yet, but were being beefed up for any contingency. Materiel was being sent to our European allies.

Everything in my training and service of the last ten years seemed like playing games. Now military life was real, military life was earnest. One could not keep the seriousness of the situation confined to the base. It came home with you.

A Career Comes into Focus

"How did things go today, darling?" Pete held a cold beer out to me. I took it, kissed her, and downed two or three deep quaffs.

"Sometimes I think that it's all getting out of hand. You wouldn't believe the detail. It boggles the mind."

She sat down beside me. "Don't you have enough bookkeeping machines and other automatic office equipment?"

"It boggles the machines, too. There's got to be a better way."

The baby started crying. "Peter, please see what's wrong with Richard," Pete called to our oldest son. Then turning back to me, she remarked, "When there's a need, somebody always comes along to fill it."

That gave me an idea. The next morning, I phoned the manager of International Business Machines. I told him about some of the problems we were having. He said his company was working on a new card system, and he later came to Wright Field to demonstrate it. IBM punch cards would soon become at least a temporary solution to our record-keeping problems.

One Sunday morning, I was working in my office to catch up on some important papers. I had the radio on. Suddenly the music stopped. A special announcement came on. The Japanese had attacked Pearl Harbor, our entire Pacific Fleet had been sunk! It was December 7, 1941.

What a shock! There had been word from Washington that there might be trouble in the Pacific; they recommended equipment in the area be reinforced. But this was a total surprise, and a horrible catastrophe.

My immediate reaction to that radio anouncement was to report for duty, alert our people, and establish communications. I called the Bell System central office and arranged to have lines opened, and kept open, between Wright Field and our seven depots. I also had a line between my office and the Pentagon.

We had materiel moving to the Pacific on that very same day.

At my first opportunity I phoned Pete. "We are at war," I predicted. "Japan has attacked Pearl Harbor. We've lost a lot of ships."

"My family," she gasped, "are they safe?"

Pete's mother and brothers all lived in Manoa Valley. "I'll try to find out," I said, "but all communication lines are tied up for priority use."

It was five days before we had a cable from her brother, Fred, saying that the entire family had escaped injury and was safe. We all breathed easier, but in the back of our minds was the unexpressed awareness that Hawaii was even more vulnerable now than before, and that the large Japanese-born population was a question mark for the Islands' safety.

The youngsters and Pete needed me more than ever. But so did the Air Corps. We were not under fire, but we were under stress. Peter and Gerry had endless questions about bombings and sinkings. What is happening, Daddy? What will happen?

I gave reassuring answers, not only to them but to Pete. Then I turned around and sought reassuring answers myself at the base.

Nobody had any answers at that time. All we knew was that the uniform now meant more than ever before. The definition of the word "duty" had expanded exponentially. The existence of the United States depended on its military forces...on me.

The United States had joined World War II.

PART II

Chapter V

At War

The attack on Pearl Harbor was an attack on me personally, though I was thousands of miles away. The many small battles I had experienced in my life were dwarfed by this enormous holocaust.

I sat that night in the living room, listening to the news with Pete. The boys had gone to bed. On the wall was a Distinguished Flying Cross for my part in the rescue of that air crew that had parachuted into the rough Hawaiian water in 1930. How unimportant it looked now. I remembered also how I had bailed out of my burning plane, over the Mexican border in 1932, and how again, in 1940, I had parachuted from a storm-battered fighter plane. Now, these hair-raising incidents became dwarfed in the immensity of Pearl Harbor.

The radio announcer was listing the names of the ships sunk and the aircraft lost. "Eighteen B-17 heavy bombers arrived in Hawaii during the attack to reinforce our air arm there, but were quickly destroyed by enemy fire as they were landing at Hickam." I remembered those planes leaving Wright Field a few days before for the West Coast.

Only yesterday, I had taken our two Chesapeake retrievers for a romp across the golf course, spotted a dove's nest a couple of fairways off, banded the nestlings, and sent the banding reports off to the appropriate agency that charted bird migration. The previous weekend I went fishing with my sons and duck hunting with a friend

Rawlings

with a friend. I had a gut feeling that these activities would at least temporarily fall victim to the war.

My days would be different. I felt a new drive welling up inside.

"A penny for your thoughts, Ed." The news had given way to music and Pete turned off the radio.

"You're wasting your money, love, you know damn well I'm thinking about the war and how it's going to affect our lives."

"Do you think they'll send you into combat?" she asked.

"They'll be mustering in so many men, there won't be planes for them to learn to fly, planes for them to fight with, or planes for them to bomb with. They'll need me at least for now to help fill those supply channels."

Pete nodded with relief. Yes, that was my expertise and it was immensely critical now.

"How can I help?" she asked.

I knew she meant this sincerely. She had fought the Battle of Harvard Business School with me and helped me to win. She was now ready for this battle, too.

"I'll have to be spending longer hours on the base. I won't be seeing you or the kids as much. You'll have to be an understanding wife and a father as well as a mother to the boys."

She came over and sat on my lap. We did the rest of our musing about the impact of the day's events — with our heads together.

I was at Wright Field office an hour early that next morning.

The base was not the beehive of activity I had envisioned. I was frustrated. The drive I felt to push harder and faster could not be expressed. Each step crying for action required some preliminary action that protocol and standard operating procedure dictated: clearances, approvals, cross-checking.

Before I tell how I reacted to this frustration at the start of World War II, let me flash ahead and tell how I reacted some seven years later when I was a Lt. General and the Air Force's first Comptroller and I was faced with a similar frustration, albeit of a different cause. Congress had made cuts in the budget that had to be implemented in the most painless, practical way. It was a problem in simple arithmetic, but it took so long to work out by hand that by the time it could be completed, there would be a new Congress and a new budget. It was clear that some mechanical means would be essential to do the job.

45

At war

It came to my attention that the Census Bureau was wrestling with the same problem — vast quantities of data that were almost impossible to handle. The Air Force and Bureau of Census began cooperating to solve this problem, but then the money they had available for this had run out. The Air Force had no such allocation of funds. Still, we just had to have that numbers manipulator.

What could I do? It was a matter of money. I went over our budget with a fine-tooth comb and spotted an account called "Industrial Planning." I reasoned that this problem involved "Industrial Planning."

Without telling the Chief of the Bureau of Census or the Secretary of the Air Force, I transferred $100,000 from that account to the Census Bureau. The effort was kept alive with these funds. As a result, after the Census Bureau got theirs, the Air Force received its first commercial computer. In fact, the Air Force got the first computer in the Department of Defense.

I relate this now to illustrate my initiative in that case. Even though I was Lt. General at that time, there was still protocol to be followed. Yet I circumvented it in the spirit of practical reality.

Now, at the outset of World War II, that same initiative had to be given full expression. Being in command of the Aircraft Production Section, Materiel Division, I had to face 8,000 shortage requests. They were put on IBM cards so that they could be pulled out by priority, by classification, and by any other characteristic that planning strategy dictated.

How these shortages were then filled demanded initiative. I could not stand by waiting for a piece of paper while the Japanese were shooting down our planes, sinking our ships, and killing our boys. I had to be a self-starter.

Using common sense, I made decisions locally that my intuition told me would be later legitimized by higher authority. It was the only way to go. I mean *really* go. Some items were in such short supply that we had to improvise. At one point, aluminum was so tight, we substituted wood in some trainers. Another example was flat tracks (aluminum forgings for ailerons on P-38 fighters), which were so tight we took other forgings out of their schedule. Even so, we had to fly them to California to keep the P-38 line going.

There were the lambs among us at Wright Field who, in the

interest of rules and regulations and the letter of military law, would have us wait, go slow, and give red tape its due. I shudder even now to think the effect this might have had on the outcome of the war. Thankfully, there were many able businessmen who enlisted after Pearl Harbor, which made manning the operation comparatively easy.

I encouraged the revving up of our depots. Existing commitments were speeded up and dates pushed forward so as to get supplies to Hawaii and the Philippines as quickly as possible. With the United States now committing their own forces to the European conflict, that theatre also had to receive accelerated supplies.

The War Production Board went into full swing. The Joint Chiefs of Staff established a priority list that became the guide for our operations. We, in turn, worked with the Aircraft Division of the War Production Board.

Who do I mean when I say "we"? An Aircraft Scheduling Unit was formed at Wright Field by the Air Corps Materiel Division, which also had a Production Division to carry out the Aircraft Scheduling Unit's instructions. These instructions were based on logistical realities that often were different than General "Hap" Arnold, head of the U.S. Army Air Corps, ordered on allocation of airplanes. Here I was a Colonel having to overrule General Arnold, a most tenuous position.

This Production Division was manned by both Air Force and Navy personnel. I was soon put in charge of this Production Division. It was then that I was confronted with those 8,000 materiel shortages.

I found an officer who had been with IBM and put him in charge of the battery of IBM equipment for processing the punch cards. With a clear-cut view of the bottlenecks, I was then able to concentrate my activities on investigating the causes of those bottlenecks and then attempting to remove them.

A slow contractor might make improved deliveries in response to a phone call or a telex or both. On the other hand, a visit might be required to troubleshoot the slow pace of deliveries and prescribe corrective steps.

These field trips were often expedited by the local Congressman whose physical presence helped to dramatize the importance of that plant's production. Of course, I had to be patient while the in-

At war

evitable speeches took place, and I had to put up with their bad jokes. Usually, we found that the plant did not have the right machine tooling, so we made recommendations to correct that, too.

Never at fault was a lack of dedication on the part of the employees. National loyalty transcended all classic labor grievances. Women augmented the work force, symbolized by Rosie The Riveter.

Production volume took off like the very planes they were producing. President Roosevelt had dared to set 50,000 planes as an annual goal. In the first year we produced 120,000 aircraft. The second year: 200,000. And I went up in rank, step by step, in just a few months.

I flew thousands of miles inspecting, expediting, perfecting. But delivering the materiel became the bottleneck, especially in the Pacific. When Japan attacked Pearl Harbor, Douglas MacArthur was our man in the Philippines. His planes were caught by surprise, just as they were at Pearl Harbor. Without air control, and poorly equipped, his troops were squeezed into defensive positions on the Bataan Peninsula and the fortified island of Corregidor in the Bay of Manila. Lt. General MacArthur's repeated calls to Washington for reinforcements and supplies went largely unmet because of the lack of defensible transport. Our Navy had been so badly battered at Pearl Harbor that now only an occasional supply submarine could get through. We in Dayton were powerless to help.

The situation in Europe was quite different. We were in control of communication lines, and our planes got delivered along with all of the materiel needed to keep them flying. So, while the war in the Pacific became a holding operation — and a disappointing one at that, the war in Europe, after D-Day, became a winning war. So great was the tidal wave of planes, tanks, ammunition, and men, Germany never had a chance.

One day, we in Dayton, received materiel requests form the Joint Chiefs of Staff that carried a higher priority than anything before.

"We have to do some shuffling," I told my staff.

"But, we'll miss schedule on these," warned one of my officers.

"Then so be it," I replied. "We must trust the judgement of the JCS."

Months later, we learned that we had been working on the Manhattan Project, helping to produce the first atomic bomb.

Rawlings

Monthly production rates were of vital interest to the Pentagon. Strategy had to be supported by the reality of logistics. The reporting procedures that I had a hand in developing, just prior to the war, now became monthly rituals.

Pete and the kids hardly saw me for the 48 hours preceding the submission of these reports and not at all on the day of submission because I took them to Washington by train. First I was driven in top secrecy to the depot. I locked myself into a stateroom with my .45 strapped to my hip. Then, on arrival in Washington, I was met by Colonel Tex Thornton. It was like a lateral pass. He ran with it the rest of the way. Tex, who later set up the Litton Company, was also a Harvard Business School graduate. He had been on Wall Street before joining the staff of Assistant Secretary for Air, Robert Lovett.

The main reason these Production Reports were so vital to the Pentagon is this: they were the basis for the allocation of aircraft between the Air Corps, the Navy, the British, the French, and the Russians. We had to do everything possible to make these reports as accurate as possible.

Material Air Transport Service (MATS) delivered all aircraft to the forces to which they were allocated, except the Russians. The Russians insisted on taking delivery themselves in Nome, Alaska. They would not let anyone fly their airspace, preferring instead to send their own crews in from Siberia to Nome. This was fine with us because they were proving themselves as a strong ally.

Occasionally I would lose my Wright Field staff members to combat duty. This would always be an emotional time, not only because I was going to miss the valuable services of some experienced and trusted colleague, but also because he was going and I was not.

I had been trying to get an overseas assignment but without success. I decided to put on some pressure, alerting Pete to the fact.

"I was born to fly, not shuffle reports," I remarked to her one evening. She knew what was coming next.

"You've made another request for overseas," she said dejectedly. "But you know how much you are needed here. Why feel guilty?"

"It's not guilt. It's a need to be where the action is. I'm a good flyer. I can make a contribution in the air over Europe just as well as at a desk in Dayton. Maybe better!"

One thing about Pete. She always expressed her contrary opin-

At war

ion, but then she always supported me in my decisions.

"When do you think you will be leaving?" she asked.

"No idea 'when,' or even 'if,'" I replied. "I just wanted to alert you to the possibility."

The when never came. My request for overseas assignment was denied on the basis that I was the only permanent officer at Wright Field, surrounded by 500 temporary officers. I was Wright Field's continuity.

But I never succumbed to routine. If my drive could not find expression behind the controls of an aircraft, it sought expression in cutting time, reducing costs, improving efficiency as my way of helping to win the war.

One improvement we were able to effect on the Supply side came as a result of the cooperative work we were doing with IBM in order to find a way to shorten the time it took to process a requisition. A requisition from Europe, for example, would normally come by mail. This could take a week. Our work with IBM produced the Transceiver. You could put a punch card in the Transceiver in Europe and it would be instantly transmitted to a punch card in Dayton, saving seven days. Translated into money, the savings in pipeline time for engines alone was $44 million.

Another innovation, suggested by one of the depots, also saved time and money. Historically, when an aircraft was damaged away from home, it had to be dismantled and towed or shipped home for repair. It was proposed that repair teams be organized who would fly to the site of the damaged aircraft, do the work on the spot, and put the plane back in service. This would not only be faster, but cheaper.

The proposal was discussed in Dayton.

"Where would the repair teams be organized?"

"At each depot."

"But they're all manned by civilians."

"So?"

"You'll never get them to fly to the damaged craft."

"Let's see what happens."

What happened was just the reverse. Civilians vied for spots on the repair teams and a chance to fly overseas. Repairs were made in both theatres more expeditiously.

Rawlings

I had each depot rated by function once a month. Their ratings then became the basis for our monthly meeting discussions. It gave each Depot Commander and Headquarters staffer the chance to address problem areas and to propose possible solutions. Some of these discussions dragged out and the meetings often became tedious. But the net result was a more open recognition of inherent problems, and a more dynamic approach to solving them.

The pressure of war proved a temptation in Procurement to circumvent the competitive bidding process. Too few bids were invited in some cases. In other cases, contracts were renewed or extended. We found the result of this to be higher costs. Prohibitive costs can contribute to the loss of a business, or of a war.

We bore down on the competitive bidding procedure. We insisted on getting as many competitive bids as possible. Soon, costs were contained.

The German army was retreating. As the end of war in that theatre became a possibility, the prospect of slowing down the whirring wheels of production that we had whipped to a frenzy now came under serious scrutiny. The Air Staff, and other branches of the military, began making plans for winding down the war.

The President and Joint Chiefs of Staff recognized that we could win the war and lose the peace, because the transition from a war economy to a peacetime economy was fraught with dangers of unemployment, depression, and economic collapse. That transition had to be made in such a way that producers of military supplies, now dependent on one customer (the government) for the bulk of their business, would not be damaged irreparably by the withdrawal of that customer.

It boiled down to terminating uncompleted contracts and disposing of tooling, raw materials, and semi-finished product. Thanks to a couple of far-sighted men, Baruch and Hancock, who wrote a report to President Roosevelt on the aftermath of World War I, the Contract Termination Act was passed by Congress to begin the massive transition. It would take some five thousand officers to implement this transition in all of the services. A school was set up in Washington for all of the services. A core of officers were trained in the proper procedures. These officers then established contract termination centers to train officers in their branch of the service in how

At war

to carry out these procedures. I was named to head readjustment for the Air Corps.

The Air Corps established two such schools, one in Vandalia, Ohio, the other at Harvard Business School. Here, readjustment officers were oriented to the legal way to notify a contractor of termination and to have him notify his subcontractors; to establish an inventory of completed product, and to estimate the percentage of completion of uncompleted inventory; and to inventory, by cost and amount, the raw materials or fabricated materials on hand awaiting use.

With this information, the readjustment officer in a particular termination could arrive at a reasonable sum for taking over the finished, semi-finished, and raw materials. Once negotiated, this sum would then have to be approved by us.

It was my responsibility to organize this critical function while at the same time keeping the supplies flowing in both theatres of war. No sooner had I recruited and trained my Readjustment Officers when the Germans struck back for the last time, in the Battle of the Bulge.

Overnight my men had to be turned from production terminators to production expediters. But we fought off the Germans at the Bulge, and now it was just a question of months. Once more, the winding down process began, and this time it was not a false start. Germany capitulated.

I was still wanting to fly so bad I could taste it. The man in charge of Army and Army Air Corps Readjustment was Secretary Royal at the Pentagon. I got an appointment to see him. The conversation went something like this:

"I'm an Air Corps man. I must fly. I've done my duty as it's been assigned to me..."

"Yes, and admirably, I must say."

"I would like to be transferred to Pacific Operations."

"But you're our key man in Readjustment, Ed. We can't get along without our only regular. The others are Johnny-come-latelys to this job."

"I lost my chance to fly in the European Theatre because I was the only regular. Does being a regular insure my always being a regular?"

Secretary Royal sensed my ennui. He looked over some papers. When he looked up, he had a smile on his face. "I can transfer you to General MacArthur, but it's on one condition."

It was now my turn to beam. "Anything you say!"

"The condition is that when the war is over, you come back to Air Corps Readjustment."

"Agreed." We shook hands.

I was overjoyed. But that joy sobered as I approached my home. It would not be easy to break the news. The boys postponed the agony by showing me their latest model airplane. After I had thrown the football with them, walked the dogs, and finished dinner, the moment had arrived.

"I've got some news."

"You're going to the Pacific," chimed in Pete.

Whatever they say about a woman's intuition, I heartily agree.

"Yes, to the Philippines."

"Is it a temporary assignment?"

"I guess you could call it that. Till the war is over and that shouldn't be too long."

I went over and sat beside her. We held hands. She turned and looked me in the eye, saying "Promise me you won't take any foolish chances."

"I already promised Secretary Royal that I'll come back here to the same old job when the war is over." She squeezed my hand and I hers.

I worked it out so that I would be in charge of Air Logistics for MacArthur. In a few days I was flown to Hamilton Field, California. While I was there waiting for my flight to Manila, two other flights were taking place, — one over Hiroshima the other over Nagasaki. The materiel I had procured under the top priority Manhattan Project had finally been delivered.

The next day, the Japanese capitulated. That ended my overseas stint during World War II. I went back to Dayton.

"That was quick," said Pete, relieved.

"Yes," I replied modestly, "they heard I was coming."

It was back to Readjustment work as usual the next day. The day the war ended in the Pacific, we had cancelled twenty billion dollars worth of undelivered contracts. I had organized teams comprised of a contracting officer, an accountant, a property disposal man, and a general cleanup man. Each team was assigned so many contracts,

Rawlings

either in numbers or in dollars, and told that when they settled those cases satisfactorily, they could go home. What an incentive that proved to be!

Now that the process had to be repeated, only on a larger scale, as the country went from all-out war to all-out peace. My orders to the Readjustment teams were to make fair settlements that would still protect the taxpayers' dollars.

The JCS orders to me were to save this country from a recession such as followed World War I. We succeeded, but the going was tough at times. One difficult aspect was the liquidation of partially completed products. Do you value at the contractor's cost or at market? We leaned in the direction of the former, but when it came time to dispose of what was now government-owned materiel, it had to be sold to the highest bidder, which frequently produced only a fraction of the settlement cost.

Furthermore, in just the way unusually high procurement costs will get unsavory publicity, selling bombers for a few thousand dollars only because they had no motors was an operation that made headlines, and I had to go before Congress to justify those kinds of surplus property disposals. Members of Congress had themselves expressed in statute the basic philosophy behind Readjustment, so they were thoroughly satisfied that their principles were being observed.

In 1947, the National Defense Act provided for the creation of the Air Force as a new and separate branch of the armed forces. I was now a two-star general in the United States Air Force. I was also approaching my twentieth year of service. Because I had continuous contact all of these years with business and industry, there were a number of companies reminding me of the twenty-year retirement law and making me some attractive offers. One came from Herb Walker, head of G. H. Walker, a New York investment banking and stock brokerage firm.

It sounded good to both me and Pete, and I decided to discuss my retirement with General Ira Eaker, Vice Chief of Staff.

"I don't have final say in the matter," he informed me. "Your retirement will have to be approved by Secretary Stuart

Symington. I'll go with you to see him now, if you'd like." Little did I know that Symington and Walker had been classmates at Yale.

Together we walked over to Secretary Symington's office. I told him of my plans to join G. H. Walker. Without a word he picked up the phone.

"Herby," I heard him say, "Ed Rawlings will not be joining you. I have just named him the first Comptroller of the Air Force."

Chapter VI

More Stars

As Comptroller, I went from Brigadier General to Major General.

My office was in the Pentagon. I lived at nearby Bolling Field with Pete and our four sons. I had come of age.

I was flying all right. But not only in planes. I had always looked up to the so-called "Top Brass." Now I was one. I rubbed shoulders with the people in the high echelons of all of the Armed Services and all branches of the federal government.

Comptroller! First Comptroller of the U.S. Air Force! I surveyed my office, my supporting staff. I sat down at my desk. I looked into the empty drawers. Now what? What does a Comptroller do? He controls the finances. That means budgets, reports, inventories. One thing about Harvard Business School: it teaches principles that have universal application. Thanks to my training there — and also thanks to the practical experience I had in wartime production and postwar readjustment — I was able to "comptroll" from my first day on the job.

By snooping around and through chats over coffee, I began to realize the top priority was *budget*. The U.S. Army Air Corps budget now became the budget of the U.S. Air Force, with some changes. Since the budgeting procedures were already in place, all I had to do was transfer those procedures to flow through my office. Flow they did. The flow of numbers became so great we were innundated. We needed to modernize. In the previous chapter I told how we used the budget to help budgeting. We found $100,000 under Industrial Planning which we transferred to Census where the same problem existed.

As a result, the first general purpose computer - a Sperry Univac 1 was put in the service of the Air Force. It was put into immediate use in Air for budgeting.

The cost of preparing the room for that computer was even more than the cost of the computer. Since it had hundreds of vacuum tubes in those days, it generated enormous amounts of heat. This heat had to be dissipated rapidly, or the tubes would break down. But that computer solved our numbers problem. It did the necessary arithmetic to bring budgets and programs into proper balance.

All through the hearings on the National Defense Bill of 1947 which separated the Air Force from the Army, the Air Force witnesses were asked over and over if they intended to duplicate the services being provided by the Army engineering, construction, finance, and medical services, etc. The answer was always, "No, we will continue to utilize existing Army services."

This promise came back to haunt us.

One morning I was called into the office of Chief of Staff General Hoyt Vandenberg.

"Ed, see these letters." He held up a large bundle of mail. "These are all from wives and mothers of our airmen in Europe. They are not receiving their allotment checks."

Having expected some problems with the function of my office, I was relieved. "That's the responsibility of the Army," I reminded him.

"Yes, I know," he said. "But Ed, you fix it."

Here was a challenge. How do you "fix" the Army's problem without taking over that function yourself? I sat at my desk mulling over that problem in the light of the intent of Congress in legislating the separation. It was a Catch-22. But I had an order to obey; I had to see to it that airmen's families received their allotment checks. If the Army's finance center was not doing the job for us, we had to have our own finance center to get the job done.

I talked over the problem with Assistant Secretary of the Air Force Gene Zuckert. I explained what I intended to do — create a separate Air Force Finance Center — and the manpower assistance

More Stars

I would need. He agreed down the line.

Maybe it was in anticipation of just such a problem, but when we had separated from the Army I was able to arrange the transfer from the Army to the Air Force of several of the best finance officers, namely Colonel Ken Webber, Jack Gilchrist, and Colonel Tom Corwin. I alerted them to the problems at hand. Then I called a Wright Field man who had been serving me well during the settlement of terminated contracts. Colonel Phagan, a CPA, said he would join me in a few days to head a finance center team.

All on that team agreed on the criteria for a finance center. It had to have good communications by air, rail, telephone, and telegraph. It had to be close to a potential supply of clerical labor. And the cost had to be minimal.

The team left on its search, and I was gratified to see them back in about two weeks with a proposed solution: a group of fine, brick warehouses in Denver, Colorado, had been declared surplus by the Army. However, the City of Denver had its eye on those buildings for municipal use. Colonel Phagan called on the mayor, then told me how that conversation went.

"Mr. Mayor, those buildings would make an ideal Air Force Finance Center."

"The City of Denver has first crack at them, Colonel, and it looks like we are going to take advantage of their availability."

"But, Mr. Mayor, you have unemployed in your city. This can be costly to you. To operate this Finance Center, the Air Force would hire some 3,000 permanent civilian employees here in Denver."

"Colonel, the City of Denver has just relinquished its need for those buildings, count on our fullest cooperation in getting them transferred to you."

Those buildings met all the criteria we set. Furthermore, the costs to modify them would be a modest $50,000. I prepared a presentation of the problem with this as a solution. I then met with the staff of the House Armed Forces Committee and won their unanimous approval. The next step was to get the concurrence of that Committee's Chairman, Carl Vinson.

Giving Mr. Vinson the briefing, I emphasized almost to the point of my own tears the poor wives and mothers who were not receiving their allotment checks.

"General, have you talked with anyone on the Hill?"

"No, I have not." I had been scrupulously careful not to.

He thought a moment, then said, "General, down in Milledgeville, Georgia, (I recognized that to be his home town) we have a hospital built by the Navy near the end of the war. It is not being adequately used by the VA. It might make a good finance center. If that is not suitable, there is a resort hotel in Savannah that the Army used as a hospital during the war. That also might be suitable."

He was a good Congressman. He was representing the interest of his constituency.

"Mr. Vinson," I replied, "I'll be on my way down there in the morning."

General Weber and I flew south in the morning. It was a beautiful hospital, one of the nicest we had ever seen. The Navy had spared no expense. It was built of brick, marble, stainless steel, copper, all critical materials during the war. The operating rooms were outfitted with the latest equipment. It had a swimming pool, green houses, tennis courts, golf courses, nursery, and flying field. What an expense to convert it to a finance center and what a waste to use it as anything but a hospital.

We proceeded to Savannah. The resort hotel was a group of old, dilapidated buildings that would have to be totally rebuilt to fit our needs. Out of the question.

When we got back to Washington, I called on Mr. Vinson.

"I have never seen such a beautiful hospital, Mr. Vinson, It would be a crying shame to cut it up for a finance center that would still be inadequate." I girded for the clincher. "You know, Mr. Vinson, the Air Force does not have a hospital. This would make a good one."

His response was an enthusiastic "General, you can have your Finance Center in Denver!"

One hand washes the other. I had learned at Harvard Business School how that principle applied in business. Now I was seeing its broader applications.

We immediately set to work to modify the warehouse and to organize the buildings to ensure an efficient flow of paperwork. When this was completed, personnel were hired, largely from the Denver

More Stars

area in accordance with our commitment to the mayor, and the Air Force was in the finance business with operations in full swing. Allotment check delays became a thing of the past.

A year after World War II ended, relations began to deteriorate between the United States and the Soviet Union's communist bloc. In 1946, Winston Churchill coined the term "iron curtain" to describe the barrier established by Soviet-controlled Eastern Europe and the Western Europe countries. The hostility came to be called the Cold War.

When specific unfriendly acts were directed at Greece and Turkey, President Truman requested an appropriation of $400 million for economic and military aid to bolster those two countries.

This principle of containment of Soviet aggression was later expanded and came to be called the Truman Doctrine. It established the United States position in the Cold War, giving the Joint Chiefs of Staff some complicated problems to solve that soon had their impact on the Air Force Comptroller's Office.

The first budgets were around $18 billion. The first step in creating a budget was receiving the requirements of the Joint Chiefs of Staff. Those were passed to the operating units of the Air Force to put a dollar figure on them. From that we would compile the budget, but only after first carefully reviewing the dollar figures submitted. Here my past experience in Dayton, first with procurement and later with termination activities, gave me a nose for these figures. They had to be sound; I had to justify them to Congress.

I was now flying more, out of Washington, and later out of Dayton, than the air hours I had logged before. But it is different than piloting your own plane. The reason for these trips was to obtain firsthand information of costs and cost-control procedures.

One flight to Alaska uncovered an unexpected drain on the taxpayer's dollars. Examining a warehouse, I noticed a huge stack of cartons.

"What's in those cartons?" I asked the officer in charge.

After prying into one of the cartons, he returned somewhat abashed.

"Well?" I asked.

"Those are boxes of Kotex, sir," he replied.

I checked his roster. "You have only one female stationed here. Do you have some other use for sanitary napkins?"

"No sir. There must have been some mistake along the line."

"Well," I replied," you better find some use." I wish I knew what he did with it all.

A number of international developments kept the United States on its military toes in the late forties and early fifties, spelling out the need for preparedness and sometimes obliterating budgets with auxiliary appropriations by Congress to cover these contingencies.

In June 1948, due to disagreemment over the status of Berlin, the Soviet Union imposed a blockade on all land transportation through the Soviet occupation zones in East Germany. Berlin was cut off from fuel, food, and other basic necessities.

The Western powers responded by creating an air corridor between these zones and staging an airlift. About 1,000 planes a day began flying supplies to the two million residents of the Western zones of Berlin.

In estimating the U.S. share of this airlift expense and handling the logistics of the massive operation, the element of time was a question mark. We had to plan month by month. Another unknown was the Soviet reaction to the airlift. Their only option to end it was to attack our planes, so we had to be prepared financially and logistically for that possibility. It would mean war.

Fortunately, the Soviets understood this. In May 1949 they offered to terminate the blockade if the three Western allies would terminate their counterblockade. So it was that some ten months after the airlift had begun and after a quarter-million flights into Berlin, normal supplies were again being transported by truck, train, and canal barge.

Thinking back some forty years later, I recall no typical day in the Office of the Comptroller. It was typical to be nontypical. New problems had to be addressed, new procedures authorized, new emergencies handled. We breathed a sigh of relief when the airlift ended, but the hiatus was to be short-lived.

* * * *

At the end of World War II, Japan was divested of Korea, which

More Stars

she had for many years claimed as a protectorate. That country was divided at the 38th north parallel for the purposes of occupation — the northern part by the Soviet Union, the southern by American troops. When there was no agreement on a plan for unification, the Soviets established a communist government in North Korea in 1948. Under supervision of the United Nations an election was held in South Korea that same year and the Republic of Korea was established with Dr. Syngman Rhee as President. The next year the last American troops were taken out by ship and air. In June 1950 North Korean troops led by Soviet-trained officers with Soviet equipment crossed the 38th parallel and began a surprise invasion of South Korea.

The United Nation's Security Council — sans the Soviet delegate — declared North Korea an aggressor and called on member nations to assist South Korea. The United Nations forces, supplied by 17 nations, were placed under the command of a man I greatly admired: General Douglas MacArthur. Once again, as during World War II, the Pentagon was on a 24-hour-a-day schedule.

Early in the Korean War, I met personally with General MacArthur. He had a special map with him which he used to illustrate his appeal to the joint Chiefs of Staff to use air power to knock out the communists.

I'll never forget that map. It showed the River Yalu in great detail, the forward line of the communists at that time. MacArthur's map showed their troop concentration, their supply depots, and the most likely spots for fording the river. All the information that a good commander would require to make a sound decision, he had delineated on that map.

He convinced the Joint Chiefs that an air strike would be a good strategic move. They gave him the go-ahead.

But then the Commander-in-Chief said no. President Truman was concerned that the Russians would enter the war if we struck from the air. Most of us disagreed.

In November, 1952, General Eisenhower was elected President of the United States. The following month he visited the Korean front, keeping a campaign promise. General MacArthur had been replaced by General Matthew B. Ridgway the year before by order of President Truman. An armistice was signed in July 1953, fixing the boundary between the two Koreas at the 38th parallel. The cost to the United States had been over 100,000 wounded in combat, over 50,000 killed, and $18 billion.

* * * *

A favorite project during my tenure as Comptroller was the establishment of the Air Force Academy. The herculean first step was, of course, getting the funds from Congress.

The original designs were quickly approved and no problems arose, until...the construction of the chapel. Then, every member of the two Congressional appropriations committees became a specialist in chapel design. The only way to solve the problem was to resist change orders and stick to the original design. Today it is one of the most beautiful buildings in the United States and there are a lot of people who claim credit for it!

I enjoyed my Comptroller's job. I enjoyed my relationships with Congress. I learned a lot. Pete did not get swept up into the fast moving social life, but preferred to be at home with the four growing boys. She began to be interested in painting and in antiques.

One afternoon when she was busy in the house, our son Gerry, then 10 years old, undertook to help the U.S. Air Force with one of its housekeeping tasks. It was common procedure to repaint and freshen up a house on the base while it was temporarily vacant. The house next door to ours was being prepared for such a repainting, and the cans of paint, brushes, etc., had been deposited on the premises. Gerry, together with General Partridge's daughter and Gen. O'Donnell's son, decided to pitch in and save the Air Force time.

When I came home that evening, I was escorted to the house to see their "handiwork." Pete and I stopped dead in our tracks. The rooms were a surrealist's nightmare. The well-intentioned youngsters had created triple work for the maintenance personnel and the shocked parents had to dig deep into their pockets to provide adequate restitution.

We had to go to Congressional appropriations committees constantly to support our budget. Congress would cut our budget five or ten million dollars and we would have to bounce back with evidence to support its reinstatement. At first this was impossible because of

More Stars

the pre-computer time lag. But with the first installation of that UNIVAC, we were more successful. General Eaker asked me to go to the Hill and get a friend of ours in the House Appropriations Committee to reinstate $40 million for spare aircraft parts that we would be needing.

Congressman George Mahon went to bat for us and succeeded in restoring those funds. He was a great friend of the Air Force. Pete and I enjoyed being with him and his wife in those years. When he passed away in 1987 I arranged for the Air Force Association to award him a plaque posthumously through his widow.

I'm glad that one incident on the Hill happened to a Navy Admiral and not to me. It was a hearing on the Navy Budget and Senator McKeller from Tennessee asked the Admiral a question. As the Admiral replied lengthily, the Senator began to nod, and actually fell asleep. Senator Bridges of New Hampshire then asked the Admiral a question. As the Admiral was replying to this second question, Senator McKeller's head hit the table and he awoke with a start. Hearing the Admiral speaking to Senator Bridges, he rapped the table with his gavel and shouted, "Young man, when I ask a question, I expect you to answer me before someone else." He then ordered the Admiral out of the room!

There is another way to spell Comptroller: Controller. In fact, that is the way my position was titled when I first took over. For a while I wondered why there was foot dragging and reticence to reply or cooperate. I did some quiet investigation and found that my title as Controller was being interpreted by commanders as one of control. They wanted no part of that. I didn't blame them. We changed the title to Comptroller. That produced another problem: nobody knew what a Comptroller was. Still, things went smoother and faster and we stayed with that.

General Hoyt Vandenberg, Air Force Chief and nephew of the great Senator Arthur Vandenberg from the State of Michigan, had been testifying with me before Congress on matters concerning Air Materiel Command. We were driving across the bridge over the Potomac on our way back to the Pentagon when he turned to me and said, "Ed, do you think you can run AMC?"

Without a moment's hesitation I replied, "Of course I can."

"Well, I'm going to give you the chance."

In about two months, Pete and I would be moving back to Dayton with our four sons. But there was a war to be fought in Korea during that transition.

One day I walked into the office of Secretary of Defense Robert McNamara. He had been one of my classmates at Harvard, a workaholic then and a workaholic in Washington.

"Bob," I told him, "your job is too big for any one man to handle."

"I'm two men, Ed," he replied.

"I believe it, but you have a lot of talent assigned to you. You ought to use it. Give yourself more time to breathe."

"There's nothing surer than getting the job done yourself," he said emphatically.

It was like pouring water on a duck's back. He did not take to my advice. But I practiced what I preached. I was constantly on the lookout for good men, and I used all the means I could think of to attract them to Washington, and then to use their expertise in the most fruitful way.

I had a function that needed filling in the Comptroller's Office and there was one man I had met who struck me as perfect for that important job. His name was Dave Burchinal and he was at Maxwell Air Force Base. I flew there and told him about the attractive position I wanted him to fill. Knowing he liked to hunt, I arranged a quail shoot. It was simple to get up to fifteen or twenty coveys a day, if you knew how. I knew how. We brought back plenty of birds. Dave was exhilarated. I hit him for a 'yes' or 'no' answer on the Pentagon job. He said 'yes.' I had won my quarry.

The postscript is this: Dave worked out well in that job, chief of a programming unit in the Comptroller's office. Just as I had hoped, he liked it and it liked him. He received a number of promotions and ended up with four stars.

I was at the Pentagon because of the speed and efficiency of Readjustment in Dayton after the war. That means I was at the Pentagon because of the efforts in Dayton of, for example, my Executive Officer there, Mort Wilner, an able Washington attorney and former quarterback at Penn. I was at the Pentagon because of one Sox McMakin, who knew how to clean out contractors' plants of excess

More Stars

material with ingenuity and expedience. I was at the Pentagon because of my personal man Thayer Tutt (President of the Palamar Foundation, which owns the Broadmoor Hotel in Colorado Springs) and others; and because of Herby Walker, New York investment banker, who had offered me a position in his firm when I was ready to retire.

These are the kinds of people who contributed to the accomplishments that were labeled as *my* personal success. It was *our* success.

If there is anything that I did that I would give myself a medal for, it is the promotion of education in the military. Not a big medal, but a small one, for there is still much to be done, despite the advances made.

This is from a speech I made to a conference of industrial and business management leaders, years before I dreamed I would be one of them myself via General Mills:

> "First, we must learn, seek out, and be receptive to new ideas — and be creatively imaginative in grasping the relationship of new knowledge to the fundamental resources of management.
>
> "Second, we must clearly keep in view the paramount importance of the human element in management.
>
> "Third, and possibly the hardest guideline to follow, is to cultivate a willingness to change. We must be willing to yield the old to the new, change our methods, and to change the very pattern of our personal thought..."

Now, back to Dayton, where on August 24, 1951, as a Lieutenant General, I took command of the United States Air Force Materiel Command.

Chapter VII

Air Logistics

A Commander's family is assigned the best of quarters. The Rawlings family was no exception. It was not long before we were settled in and saying hello to old friends on the base and off.

What I had in effect created and managed as Comptroller at the Pentagon, I was now in charge of in Dayton. In reality, it was a business. The buying and logistics arm of the U.S. Air Force was a business thousands of times larger than the Dayton Company I had worked for 21 years before. In fact, it was the largest business in the world.

The object of that business was to keep the combat forces equipped for action at all times. Supplies had to be procured, stored, and maintained so that they would be easily accessible and at strategic locations, ready to meet any emergency.

And that, with apologies to Webster, is the definition of Air Force Logistics. Logistics is basically a system. But it is not a system for system's sake; it is a system sired by necessity. In this case, the necessity was the survival of our country on a planet of potential dangers.

General Hoyt Vandenburg was an expert at recognizing a job's requirements and a person's capacities, and then matching the two. It was a talent that I admired and attempted to cultivate in carrying

Air Logistics

out my own military duties. And it was a talent he carried out in naming me to this duty because it called on all of the knowledge and experience I had acquired at Hamline, at Harvard, and as contract terminator and Comptroller.

This is not to say that it came easily to me. Every day brought new challenges that required daring approaches, often putting my neck on the line.

There were 200,000 people under the Air Materiel Command when I took over. Of these, 175,000 were civilians and 25,000 military. The military included 5,000 officers and the rest airmen.

Incidentally, the airmen were mostly in our Atomic Weapon Storage activity under the command of Major General Harry Porter. I imposed severe inspections in this sensitive area, and they passed every one of these inspections with flying colors.

The preponderance of civilians in the Command presented a problem — they were really running the place. If they did not approve of what the military personnel wanted done, they just sat on their hands and did nothing, until another Commander came along who might see things their way. Give an order to an Air Force officer or airman and that order was carried out. On the other hand, give an order to a Civil Service employee in those days and he or she just sat on tenure and protected job status.

As I came up with ideas to improve the procedures of the Air Materiel Command, I began to feel the pinch of this civilian problem. Orders were not being implemented. I called in the Personnel Officer, Colonel Julian Bowman, a man I knew to be an expert in Civil Service rules and regulations.

"Julian," I said, "as you know, civil servants are anything but servants on this Base. They are obstructors. What can we do about it?"

"Not much, General," he replied. "You know how well they are protected by law."

"It's how well you know that law, Julian, that could provide an answer. I want you to study the rules, regulations, and legal interpretations and come up with a solution."

"What kind of a solution, General?"

"It has to be a solution that circumvents existing civilian control of this installation in a legal matter with minimal harm to affected families."

"Quite an order, General. I'll dig in. When do you need my answer?"

"Yesterday." He left.

Colonel Bowman returned in a few days. I stopped whatever I was in the middle of doing.

"Do you have a solution, Colonel?" I asked. It was a critical moment because much of the efficacy of my Command depended on the answer.

"I do, General, and it's a simple one," he replied. "All we do is move operating units to the field. Civilians have to go along. If they don't, then the only two options are to retire or to take a similar opening in Headquarters. Otherwise, they are out of a job."

"Is it legal?" I asked.

He pulled out some papers and recited a chapter and verse. It was legal.

"Give me an example," I replied. "Take Engine Management, for instance."

"Transfer your Engine Manager operation to Oklahoma City, say, or San Antonio. The people who are here in it have to go with it. If they decide not to relocate, they lose their jobs, retire, or, if possible, find an equivalent job."

"It sounds like you've got it, Julian," I exclaimed with jubilation. The rest of that meeting we went over the details, the steps that would have to be taken before and after, and we set a date.

When that day arrived, in one fell swoop we decentralized. All hell broke loose! When the dust cleared, we had a more compact, efficient, and responsive Air Materiel Command.

Actually, the depots to which we transferred the activities according to their functional fit were happy to have them: San Bernadino, Sacramento, Ogden, San Antonio, Oklahoma City, Mobile, Warner-Robbins.

I was then able to exercise my Command in full. Our major job was to give full logistic support to the combat forces, the 8th Air Force and SAC being our top priority.

After providing our forces in Europe with adequate numbers of aircraft, we began the task of re-equipping SAC with its first numbers of jet aircraft. Logistics was further complicated by this transition. The impact of the jet age was felt by budgets, time schedules,

Air Logistics

and strategies. It was done without a hitch.

One day, Pete pinned a fourth star on my shoulders.

In Europe, the North Atlantic Treaty Organization (NATO), formally signed in 1950, was now being implemented. NATO's headquarters were set up in Paris, and several military commands were set up. The first Supreme Allied Commander in Europe was General Dwight D. Eisenhower.

A few months after I took command, the Chinese Communists crossed the Manchurian border into North Korea, and the second year of the Korean War took on new fury. General MacArthur had to accelerate his own logistical requirements. There was an interesting sidelight back home which could be labeled "greed."

When the Korean War broke out the Air Force immediately came up with plans for six technical schools to train the thousands of recruits that had to be skilled in radio, photography, radar, engines and airframes. I said, "Let's put one in the North. We have always gone South mainly because they want us, but also because it cost less both to build and to operate. So let us put an electronic school in Minneapolis." I had the engineers check and they found that by using old Fort Snelling we could save $20,000,000. Our budget went to Congress that way and, as all Korean War budgets, sailed right through. We had $100,000,000 appropriated for the Minneapolis school.

We then started to get objections from Minneapolis. There would be too much air traffic at Wold-Chamberlin (actually very little flying would be involved). It seems that the airport manager had figured out that there was a way to get a new airport for the Twin Cities, to be paid for by Uncle Sam. The objections grew and held up the program.

We had a meeting in Secretary of Air Symington's office with Mr. Symington, General Vandenberg, Chief of Air Staff and me. After considerable discussion Secretary Symington said, "We will not build this school in Minneapolis." He also told me that since it was my idea that I could advise the Minnesota delegation of this decision.

This was a difficult assignment but fortunately I found that the Minnesota Chamber of Commerce was holding a dinner meeting two nights later. I got myself invited. Senators Humphrey and Thye plus several Congressmen were also there. My turn to speak came after the Senators had spoken.

I arose and told them that I was going to tell them what GREED could do to one. I told them of all the objections that had been coming and that the day before Secretary Symington had decided we would not build in Minneapolis though we had an appropriation of $100,000,000 in hand. I then sat down.

You could have heard a pin drop.

If the school would have been built in Minneapolis, it would have drawn many businesses. One hundred thousand men would have gone through the school each year. The permanent party would have been eight thousand civilians. What a boost that would have been to the Minneapolis economy. Uncle Sam was not going to build a new airport that would not only not save $20,000,000 by using old Fort Snelling, but would have cost an additional $20,000,000.

The moral of this story is, don't be too GREEDY.

Air Materiel Command rolled with the punches that these developments made, while at the same time cutting requisition processing time, production time, and delivery time. We initiated new reporting procedures that gave more officers a chance to express their innovative ideas, needs, and money-saving suggestions. This was during General Curtis LeMay's tenure. I arranged for monthly meetings between my staff and his at his headquarters in Omaha. These communications paid off handsomely.

The Air Force was behaving as a business — competitive, economic, communicative, innovative, and efficient. In fact, private businesses that had to deal with the Air Force began to become aware of the Air Force's own business skills. I and some of my colleagues began to be invited to speak at business meetings, seminars, and conventions. I began to receive citations, awards, and honorary degrees. It was an exhilarating period in my life. But not without its dangers.

One day I flew back from Detroit after having given a talk before a meeting of automotive executives. Three of us rode in a B-17 piloted by Captain "Steve" Stevens.

As we approached Wright-Patterson Field, the pilot put the wing flaps down to come in for a landing. At that moment, the far right-hand motor of the four-engine bomber caught fire. Flames streaked 100 feet behind the plane. We steeled ourselves for the landing and a quick exit.

Air Logistics

Steve brought the fiery plane down on the runway with a distinct 'kaplunk.' Now the flames were shooting straight up. We climbed out of the plane and moved quickly away, expecting an explosion of the gas tanks at any moment. I could hear the fire engines on their way.

I looked for Steve. We were all accounted for except him.

"Where's Steve?" I shouted. Automatically I headed back to the burning plane. I found him beneath it. He had crawled out onto the wing, jumped off, and broken a kneecap. He was immobilized. Another officer joined me, and we picked him up and carried him to the side, at a safe distance from a plane which should have exploded by then, but had not. The firefighters sprayed foam on the fire in time.

Fortunately, Pete had not heard of the incident when I got home, so was not subjected to any fright. There I was, hale, hearty, and unscathed.

A month later, Air Secretary Harold E. Talbott in Washington awarded me the Soldier's Medal.

* * * *

The process procurement was a ticklish one. The standard operating procedure called for at least three competitive bids. Exceptions were allowed only in the rare instance when there just were not three separate suppliers available.

At times the system was being abused. Not the kind of abuse that has made modern headlines, with monkey wrenches and toilet seats costing hundreds of dollars. But not enough effort was being made to find a second or third bidder, or even a tenth or eleventh bidder, if that many suppliers were available.

I had to put the pressure on. It took guts for me to accuse top officers of being slipshod or taking short cuts. I did it, and I kept doing it, and I got no medal for it. But I got results.

Noncompetitive bids inevitably resulted in higher costs. When the competitive factor was injected more forcibly into the bidding process, costs came down. When costs came down, our budget requests became more credible. Congressmen sensed that we knew what we were talking about.

By 1952 it had become obvious that the decentralization we

had undergone to circumvent the civilian problem was creating additional benefits. Bigness can be a disadvantage to management. It can spawn so many problems that management can get bogged down in that very bigness. Decentralization, by putting operations into the field, made it possible for us at the Center to break down workloads into more manageable segments. Thus, top management was free to do its overall job of managing.

Let me tick off some of the other highlights of 1952 in Air Materiel Command:

• The AMC Management Evaluation System was devised to measure the relative standings of the AMAs and depots in selected management areas. It provided the data for us to determine if follow-up action was required.

• The first Executive Control Meeting was held in May. My purpose in inaugurating these meetings of field commanders and key headquarters people was to find out how AMC was operating and to identify deficiencies. There was no whitewashing at these meetings. Those attending understood that I was not out to make heads roll, that I appreciated frankness about shortcomings so that I could take direct action to correct them.

• The AMC Executive Development Program got under way. Provisions were made for career officers to continue their education at approved institutions. The benefits that education brought me instilled in me a drive to encourage others to seek further education, a drive that has never left me and to which I still respond today.

• A Hi-Valu program was initiated for the selective management of expensive items. Equal control by management over all items had a weak spot here. I invoked the "management by exception" principle to provide special cost and quality control over high-cost items.

• We began direct support to NATO areas. My thrust was to pare away at pipeline time — the shorter, the more effective the support, and the less the cost.

• Another thrust was to standardize logistic operations. Certain variables were fixed, unknown factors were assumed, and logistic calculations therefore simplified, pending any major changes in the current situation.

• We formed Weapon System Phasing Groups to satisfy a need created by the introduction of major new weapon systems. This was

Air Logistics

the beginning of the jet age, to be followed quickly by the space age. As each new weapon system was adopted, not only did it entail fresh production difficulties and support problems, but we had to address the phasing in of the new and the phasing out of the old. The Groups were formed to handle these particular responsibilities.

• IRAN was born: Inspect and Repair As Necessary. Naturally, all of AMC's "customers" wanted the latest and the best as soon as possible. If funds were unlimited, we would be only too happy to oblige. But, because funds were tightly budgeted and controlled, existing equipment had to make do as long as it was serviceable. We inspected and repaired, if feasible, before replacing.

• We developed a Bench Check to provide more economical field maintenance activities, many of which were devoted to minor repairs of unserviceable accessory equipment.

• Local purchasing began. AMC made low-cost item purchasing procedures more flexible. We needed to keep major acquisitions under tight control, but this made the purchase of low-dollar, small-quantity items cumbersome. We introduced several alternate purchasing procedures and contracting forms specifically designed to simplify these smaller operations while maintaining the same "lowest cost" principle.

Thankfully, a Commmanding General of AMC is not confined to such matters. There was a diversity of other responsibilities, such as parades, inspections, awards and promotions ceremonies, and, of course, hosting visiting dignitaries. Wright-Patterson received more than its share of these, as we drew from Congress, the Pentagon, industry, and even other countries, such as in 1952 when we received Lieutenant General Wang Shu-Ming, Commanding General of the Chinese Nationalist Air Force.

* * * *

Christmas always gave me a time for strengthening of family ties, often frayed by the exigencies of my job.

One Christmas we had been invited to go down to Stuttgart in Arkansas, where there was a beautiful duck camp. It was built on the edge of a large reservoir that held water to be pumped into the rice fields in the spring. Pete opted to stay home and take care of the plants and the animals. We kept the whole venture a secret from the boys until Christmas Day.

The fire was lit in our cozy fireplace. The Christmas tree was decorated. I tied four cords from various parts of the room to the tree. At the end of each cord, I tied a card saying, "Free ride to Stuttgart, Arkansas, for duck hunting." When we finished a beautiful Christmas dinner, I invited the boys to select a cord and follow it to their card.

One by one they gave a shout of joy. I had a Ford station wagon. We loaded it with our hunting gear and two sleeping bags. It was 800 miles to Stuttgart and we decided to drive straight through. Yes, my four sons were now all old enough to drive, so we took turns driving and sleeping.

The roads were excellent and there was little traffic at night. We arrived in Stuttgart just as it was getting light. We got our out-of-state hunting licenses and were soon headquartered at the pin oak reservoirs. What a wonderful week of hunting and father-sons camaraderie we had! When we returned home to Ohio we talked about it for a long time afterwards.

The years 1953 and 1954 produced no diplomatic surprises or emergencies, and they could have been years of "business as usual" in Dayton. But I feel that, if you stand still, you lose ground.

I acquired a Vice Commander in June of 1953, Major General McKee. With this additional backup, I pushed with renewed effort for increased attention to organizational efficiency. We replaced directors' meetings with an AMC Council, designed to consider Command problems in a more organized way. The Council gave the Commander carefully studied recommendations for his approval. It also worked to bring key staffers closer together.

We tried out new lines of command, shifting the organizational status of Air Force Depots and Air Procurement Districts. We changed to a dollars mode of measuring assets and activities after intensive testing showed it to be a more accurate yardstick than the quantitative one we were using. Called Monetary Inventory Accounting, it was later adopted for use throughout the Command.

Early in 1954 we got UNIVAC II. General of the Army Douglas MacArthur, now Chairman of the Board of Remington Rand, came to AMC Headquarters to dedicate this latest and most sophisticated

Air Logistics
computer.

This electronic data processing equipment became my pride and joy. Put into general use, it translated voluminous detail into manageable terms and added unprecedented speed and flexibility to our logistic operations. It was like adding a brain to one's own brain. I was continually dreaming up new uses for this electronic genius.

When logistics becomes affected by technological advances, such as the jet engine, the manual handling of the mathematical calculations needed to revise the levels of production and supply become monumental.

For instance, today's top-secret Stealth fighter, which foils radar protection, has been reported in the press to be ready for worldwide deployment. If so, it must be equipped with the most up-to-date weaponry, including "SMART" missiles, and suitable storage facilities need to be constructed to hide and protect the aircraft in strategic locations. Here is a problem in logistics that today's electronic data processing equipment will be harnessed to help solve.

We had plenty of problems arise for which we were thankful to have UNIVAC II. The computer age has kept up with the electronic age, the jet age, and the space age. In fact, their respective rates of progress are interdependent. Microcircuits now make compact computers that are so sophisticated they make UNIVAC II seem like the horse and buggy.

Harvard Business School did not teach me how to use computers. They did not exist then. Of course, computer applications in business are now very much a part of Harvard's curriculum. My exposure to this marvelous mechanism for management, first in the Pentagon and then in Dayton, was frustrated by that lack of education in computers. It had to be compensated for on the site, with the help, first of IBM and then of other suppliers.

I have always remembered that frustration, and later in this book I will explain what I have been doing to make computer literacy a prerequisite to graduation from today's major universities.

Let me give some relief from the technical aspects of my work at Dayton by describing my office.

It was a spacious ground-floor room in the stone gray rectangle of structures that housed Headquarters of AMC at Wright-Patterson. The office was walnut-paneled and I sat behind a walnut desk.

On one wall were autographed photographs of Defense Department Assistant Secretary Quarles; USAF Assistant Secretaries Sharp and Garlock; Generals Twining, LeMay, and White; and President Eisenhower.

Across the room on the facing wall were three watercolors by my wife, Pete, all of Hawaiian scenes. There was a map of the world, a globe, and a table for my trophies and plaques on which I also kept a rotating display of models of weapon systems that my Command was procuring and maintaining.

I did not go to that office in the morning until I had a brisk walk at sunrise with my two Chesapeake retrievers, Molly and Chocolate. They loved to romp on the Wright-Pat golf course or go along the tree-lined streets adjacent to the field. The neighbors might have heard a whistle blow as I occasionally put them through the hunting paces they had become adept at.

Back at Headquarters, I enjoyed a pipe. I smoked a pipe constantly, filling it each time only halfway with Bond Street tobacco.

They called me "Big Ed" but never in my presence. They may well have called me other names too, behind my back, but those did not get into print.

It was said of me that if an officer does a job I assign to him, I never forget it. I'm inclined to agree with that. I was always searching for the people who could handle more, so I could give them more to do.

It was also said of me that I had the ability to strike straight to the heart of a matter. One young officer was quoted as saying, "Whenever he asks you to brief him on a matter of importance, you'd better know the subject thoroughly. If you don't, his first question will invariably be the one you can't answer."

I usually arrived in the office at 8 A.M. The first order of the day was to attack the letters, memos, and reports already stacked on my desk by my small personal staff. Some just needed my initials as acknowledgment; others needed a penciled notation by me to a staff officer for action; still others might need a more formal dictated reply.

I never ignored the newspapers, technical reports, magazines, or other publications that were waiting for me. I had an instinct for

Air Logistics

spotting the essence that was relevant to me.

By 10 A.M. I was ready for presentations or reports by staff officers or key civilians. Usually by then my coat would be off and my sleeves rolled up. This was decision-making time, and my pipe went at double the pace. There were frequent interruptions by the phone on my desk, which was a direct line to the Pentagon.

Sometimes I had a relaxing steam bath before lunch. Then after about a half hour in the executive dining room I was back at my desk for more conferences and paperwork.

This routine was frequently broken by speaking engagements. I tried to accept invitations to civic groups, but received three times as many as I could handle. I gave Dayton groups preference over out-of-towners because Wright-Patterson was in Dayton's backyard. I had to keep our community relations and goodwill at a high level.

I tried not to play favorites. I spoke to everyone from the Girl Scouts to the American Rocket Society. I appeared in parades, at banquets, and at conferences and conventions.

A proud grandmother Rawlings poses with young Edwin as he displays that "Born to Fly" look in his eye. 1908.

Future General Edwin Rawlings, Tracy, Minnesota.

Ella Mae and Frank Rawlings, parents of Ed, Florence and Marcella are pictured in a classic pose, circa. 1900.

An early picture of the future General as he arrives in Honolulu. March 21, 1932. Note gardenia lei.

Rawlings family gathering: (l. to r.) Florence, father Frank, Marcella, Edwin, mother Ella Mae.

Young Lt. Rawlings with his Loening Amphibian. The plane is similar to the one he later landed in the Pacific to help pick up three airmen who had parachuted from their own crippled plane. The year was 1930.

Newlyweds Lt. E.W. and Muriel (Pete) Peterson Rawlings. Hawaii, July 17, 1930.

General Rawlings being escorted to dinner by the Royal Canadian Airforce Bagpipers. Ottawa, Canada.

Swedish troops are reviewed in Stockholm (1962), by General Ed Rawlings and the Chief of Sweden's Air Force.

The first Air Staff of the U.S. Air Force, 1948: (l. to r.) Generals Lauris Norstad, Muir Fairchild, William McKee, Idwald Edwards, Howard Craig, Edwin Rawlings.

General Rawlings with his boyhood friend and classmate, Dr. Lauren Donaldson, receiving honorary doctorate degrees from Hamline University.

Center stage in 1961 is General Rawlings receiving his honorary doctor of laws degree from Ohio Wesleyan University.

Throwing the first pass for "Touchdown '67", one of many successful General Mills sales contests.

The General, now the President of General Mills, makes the cover of Business Week magazine. December 9, 1961.

General Rawlings and General Mills Chairman of the Board, Charles Bell, in discussion.

In civilian "uniform" with: (l. to r.) General Alfred Gruenther, J. P. McFarland and Sewall Andrews. 1962.

J. W. Haun, S. F. Keating, J. P. McFarland, E. W. Rawlings. General Mills' Lancaster, Ohio, plant.

And he cooks too! Proof of the General's qualification as chief of General Mills.

General Mills management session: (l. to r.) L. F. Polk, D. Wright, D. A. Stevens, E. W. Rawlings, C. H. Bell, E. K. Thode, E. O. Boyer.

Business as usual on the General Mills' Jetstar.

Mayor C. Miller presenting "gold-plated" shovel to General Rawlings at Lancaster, Ohio plant. 1965.

General Mills marketing session: (l. to r.) Bill Cash, Jim Isham, L. H. Crites, Paul Harper, J. P. McFarland, J. S. Fish with General Rawlings.

General Rawlings, Bill Lohman and Bill Feighner. 1958.

Left to right...Chuck Denny, president of Magnetic Controls, Inc., along with T. R. Anderson and Ed Rawlings, directors.

The General with son, John, on Alaskan salmon fishing trip.

R & R time plus a bit of fishing at Golden Hour Lodge, Alaska.

The General with sons Peter, Gerry, John and Dick on hunting safari. Henry's Lake, Idaho. 1978.

Ed with his Chesapeake Bay retriever, Chocolate.

The General and Pete with Honey.

Russell Tutt and the General admire Air Force Academy falcon.

Sons Peter, Charles (Gerry), Richard (Dick) and John with Muriel (Pete) and the General.

The Rawlings grandchildren: Scott, Todd, Lynn, Kelly, Wendy, Robin, Douglas and Greg with Pete and the General. 1980.

Family portrait: 50th wedding anniversary.

The General in Abbott Northwestern hospital, Minneapolis, keeps up with the world while recovering from a serious operation.

Pete's brother, Robert Peterson, with the General's sister, Marcella, and her husband, Adolph Shing. 1980.

Big brother Ed Rawlings flanked by his two sisters: (l. to r.) Florence and Marcella.

Newlyweds, Edwin and Kathryn Fradkin Rawlings,
October 10, 1986.

Kathy and Ed, the newest members of Hell's Angels.

Kathy and Ed back at the ranch. 1987.

Senator Rudy Boschwitz (R-MN), General Rawlings, former senator Howard Baker (present White House Chief of Staff).

General Jack Gregory, Pacific Air Force commander, presented Air Force Exceptional Service Award to General Rawlings. February, 1987.

AFA Convention: (l. to r.) Major Paul Markgraf, General Rawlings, Senator Dave Durenberger (R-MN), Earl Rogers.

The General with his Commander-in-Chief, President Ronald Reagan.

Vice-President George Bush, General Rawlings.

Chapter VIII

A Military Career Ends

We are now in the year 1955, the beginning of the last four years of my military service.

The U.S. has signed a treaty with Nationalist China providing for mutual aid for the defense of Taiwan and the nearby Pescadores Islands. In 1956 Britain and France invaded Egypt and were forced by the United Nations to withdraw. This led in 1957 to the Eisenhower Doctrine, for which Congress appropriated funds to provide economic and military assistance to Middle East countries to help them resist communist aggression.

All of this kept a high level of logistic planning going on at Dayton, and the function of management became more demanding than ever.

People all over the world were realizing the proximity of total destruction. The atomic age was upon us. Nowhere was this realized more than at the heart of logistics for the U.S. Air Force — namely, my office.

On one of my frequent visits to speak at my alma mater, Hamline University, I expressed my concern with these words:

> "None of us can deny that perhaps mankind now possesses the weapons with which to destroy himself. But it is my own conviction that the intelligence which can create such weapons can and must learn in time

A Military Career Ends

to control its genius for good rather than evil. This is the test of our time. It is the test of education and of our universities, which bridge the gap between the accumulated wisdom of the race and the terrible and beautiful raw potentialities of the air age.

"We need from our universities, today, specialists in every field to help us realize the great potentialities of flight. But the crying need of our age and of our world is for *whole* men with the breadth and maturity to use their skills and their knowledge wisely. I hope that our universities can help teach people all over the world Christian humanism and the ability to live in tolerance, understanding, and peace with our fellows. I hope that they can teach us to settle with justice and humanity the frontiers which our minds discover — whether they be in the cold twilight of space, or within the breathable atmospheres of our homes."

The campaign that was never finished, even after I retired, was the effort to encourage the unending education of rising young Air Force officers — the generals and commanders of the future.

Pete supported me in this effort, and in many other "campaigns." She was a talented, resourceful, and understanding woman without whom I cannot conceive of my success being even a fraction of what it was. She always found time for my interests over and above the demands of the four boys, and for her own pursuits.

Her art was becoming better and better. She was a pro. We both began collecting art as well, and her pieces held their own alongside the recognized names. She joined an art club and later became head of it.

We both began to take an interest in antiques. Our boys were now away at school much of the time — Andover and Deerfield preparatory schools in Massachusetts, and our oldest, Peter, at Miami University in Ohio. Incidentally, all four later entered the Air Force, three making captain at the same time. You might say I produced not only materiel but also personnel.

Looking for antiques was a treasure hunt. You never knew when you would acquire a "find" for practically nothing. But our greatest

Rawlings

"find" was a gift to Pete. An old abondoned house built in the Civil War was slated to be torn down by the owners. Pete knew the daugher, who told her she could have anything she could cart away from this house, as a gift.

The Harries House was solidly built in the style typical of that era. The interior wood was black walnut, including a handsome spiral staircase and bannister. Pete and I knew exactly what we wanted: 13 foot-high dining room doors, 2½ inches thick, with beautiful etched glass panels.

We dismantled those four doors and loaded them on our car, together with an elegant marble sink that we just could not pass up. We gave those doors to the Officers Club at Wright Field, an impressive addition to the interior decor. Not too much later, I noticed that somebody had placed drapes over those beautiful doors! That started (albeit more localized) another Civil War.

There had been another "Civil War" raging in the area ever since Wright-Patterson was designated the Air Force's Air Materiel Command. Dayton once considered Wright-Patterson incompatible with its own future. I've mentioned how I accepted speaking engagements whenever offered from Dayton civic organizations in an effort to improve relations. These talks were just part of the total communications effort to get Dayton to understand and respect Wright-Patterson and vice versa. That respect soon began to be manifested in a switch from letters and phone calls of complaint to the presentation of citations and awards. Dayton's International Rotary Club called my efforts "Community Citizenship," and there were similar references made in awards by the Dayton Junior Chamber and Chamber of Commerce.

I mention this to make a point: most military men know the capability of war for destruction better than do most civilians. We want peace. But peace in the world must start with peace within oneself, one's family, and one's community.

* * * *

On December 17, 1957, at exactly 12:38 p.m., the Air Force fired its first Inter-Continental Ballistic Missile (ICBM). It was officially called the Atlas. We called her "Big Annie." On that day the

A Military Career Ends

Air Force entered the Space Age.

One year and one day later, on December 18, 1958, the Atlas was successfully fired into an orbit around the earth. The Air Force moved its missile program forward rapidly, expanding the frontiers of space exploration and sending reverberations into the heart of logistics and planning.

In the eight years that I had been in command of AMC, the volume of materiel we were charged with handling had increased exponentially. The basic logistic principles by which we operated, and which I had originally promulgated, were still sound; but they were so enlarged and extended that their implementation required more manpower, mor expertise, and more data processing equipment.

All of those "mores" could not be properly coordinated without another "more" — more communications. Diverse elements of the Command had to be fused into a compact, functioning unity. There had to be more base-touching and more effective interactions. We started a Base magazine in 1957, *AMC Worldwide* which briefed the command and treated everybody to a bird's-eye view. This was but one step we took in the improvement of internal and external communications.

Streamlining the organization also helps to streamline communications. In 1957 we began the phase-down of overseas depots because modern transportation and communications made direct support possible: the world was getting smaller. In 1958 an improved Pacific Logistics Plan was approved for a similar partial phase-out of Pacific depots.

In that year I also directed that each ZIAMA (Zone Interior - Air Materiel Area) set up a Directorate of Logistics Support Management, the purpose of which was to separate the management of local industrial operations from the worldwide management of weapon systems and support systems.

During this time I received the General William E. Mitchell award for outstanding contribution to aviation progress, and Honorary Doctorate degrees from a number of universities, including Miami, Dayton, Hamline, Ohio Wesleyan, Hendrix, and Tufts. I must have been doing something right.

Vice Commander McKee, who was a Major General when he

joined me in June, 1953, was promoted to Lieutenant General in 1957. He was doing everything right. I could leave the Base in his hands whenever meetings, conferences, or inspections took me out of town. And never once did I have to rescind any of his decisions. Good staffers deserve a piece of my awards.

Brigadier General Fritz Borum was the most innovative of my Depot Commanders. He decided it was taking too much time to process packages and boxes, so he mechanized the whole line. Part of it was a sawing rig that took the top off a box in seconds. His system was copied by the other six depots.

I was approaching my thirtieth year of service. The dynamic system of air logistics that I had created was not dependent on me. It was designed to stand on its own feet, no matter who was in command.

In talks at home with Pete, the subject of my career surfaced frequently. Thirty years of service seemed a good milestone. Also, from the point of view of getting a post in the industrial or commercial world after retirement, mid-fifties was a good age, at sixty or older the large corporations are hesitant to invest in your expertise.

One evening Charles Bell of General Mills, headquartered in Minneapolis, came to our house. He offered me the job of chief financial officer, a vice presidency, for that company.

He outlined the job, the remuneration, and the prospects. Then, instead of waiting for my decision, he turned to Pete.

"Would you like to come to Minneapolis?" he asked her.

Without a moment of hesitation, she replied, "Whatever Ed decides to do, I'll be happy to do." Our mutual happiness was that closely interwoven. I decided to accept.

When I had first reported to Wright Field in 1935, I was the most junior of the 100 officers on the base. When I retired 24 years later, I was the Senior Officer.

* * * *

I am frequently asked now and was asked then at functions prior to my retirement what was the most significant event in my military career. That's hard to answer. It has to be divided into categories of significance, and even then there are conflicting gauges. When I

A Military Career Ends

made my first solo flight I was so exhilarated by the significance of that event that it took me a while for me to get both feet back on the ground. But looking back now — what else is new?

Suppose I divide significant events into flying, Air Force Comptroller, and AMC categories. Here goes. First, flying:

In the summer of 1939 I was assigned a Consolidated PB-1, a two-seater experimental fighter, to fly to Boston. I took off and landed in Buffalo en route. The weather reports were favorable and I took off again for Boston. I had to fly over the Finger Lakes, known for their sudden outbursts of bad weather. A storm suddenly enveloped me. Three placards in the cabin reminded me of this plane's wicked reputation — "If in half a turn of a spin, jump!" Two test pilots had already been killed in similar planes.

Suddenly, in the middle of the storm, the plane started to spin. I jerked open the canopy and went over the side in a blinding rainstorm. A few swings of the parachute and I hit the ground, the wet chute collapsing beside me. I was already a member of the Caterpillar Club — airmen who had saved themselves by parachuting — and now it had happened again.

I gathered my chute and headed for the road. A farmer and his family driving by slowed up.

"Want to see the airplane wreck?"

"I'm the pilot. Sure, let's go." I climbed in. They stared at me like I was from outer space.

As we pulled over the hill toward Route 20, I saw an ambulance on the road and two men carrying a stretcher up the hill towards the wreck.

"Hey, here I am," I called. "I was the only one aboard."

They came over to the car and made sure I was okay. They drove me from Cherry Valley back to Buffalo where I checked into a hotel and called Wright Field. They said they would send a plane for me in the morning. Meanwhile, my right shoulder had begun to ache so I soaked in a tub of hot water.

Back home the next day, the doctor determined that I had broken my shoulder. When I'd jerked open the canopy, the severe tension had caused the tendon to pull out a piece of bone the size of a half dollar. I was taped and immobilized. By coincidence, my son, Gerry, had just broken his collarbone in play and was also taped up. Looking back at this synchronization and at my subsequent career in the business end of the Air Force, I wonder if the significance of this event might have been that I was born to fly more mentally than physically.

As for being Comptroller, the most significant event had to do with data processing.

Just why I deem it significant will be the subject of some musings and misgivings in Part IV.

Also significant was the birth of GI insurance. During World War II it was impossible for military personnel to obtain life insurance. When lives were lost, many widows and mothers were being left penniless. The Services were scrambling to find a solution.

Finally, General Kaston, Chief of Finance, U.S. Army, came up with a solution. General Eisenhower called a staff meeting to consider it. At that meeting I represented the Air Force at General Spaatz's request.

A Colonel Green, former insurance man now working with Kaston, made a good presentation and indicated they had selected a California company.

"How was this company selected?" I asked.

"We know it to be a good, reliable company," he replied.

This did not satisfy me. When the meeting was over, I called an old friend, Mort Wilner, who had worked with me during the War and who had been an insurance man before the war. He agreed: excellent program, company selection wrong.

I got word to General Eisenhower and we went out for competitive bids, against General Kaston's wishes. We received better bids. The winner was John Hancock, and we selected them to be the insurance carrier for the Air Force.

During the first few weeks there were ten deaths in the Services. John Hancock paid the beneficiaries in each case within a week, which we considered excellent service. The Armed Forces Relief and Benefit Association was in full operation. I began to hear rumors to the effect that we were competing with old-line insurance companies. This was patently false. Our carrier was an old-line company.

One day I had a call from the House Armed Forces Committee asking me to come and testify about our insurance company. At the hearing I showed the committee members how those ten cases

A Military Career Ends

had been settled within a week. The meeting ended with the Chairman praising me for the job we were doing for the survivors.

I later learned that Colonel Green had spread the rumors that had led to that investigation, and that he would get a cut from his insurance company for each insured.

I named General Kaston as the president of our Hancock agency and addressed him to be careful in the conduct of the business and to remain apart from any other activity. Soon after, I learned at a board meeting that he was organizing another company. The board agreed I should fire Kaston. I called him in and summarily did so. His wife, who had been waiting with him outside the boardroom, entered and began to castigate us. I have never heard of any other four-star general who was subjected to that kind of bombardment, but I survived.

Admiral Lyon was placed in charge. The membership grew, claims continued to be processed rapidly, and part of members' premiums have been returned as "dividends." The company is still going strong and has been able to increase coverage without an increase in premium. A significant event in more than one way, as most will agree.

There is no question in my mind that the most significant accomplishment for AMC in Dayton was decentralization. First it was decentralization that wrested control from civilians. Then it was decentralization that improved the efficiency of management throughout AMC. In 1958 the creation of AMC Aeronautical Systems Center and of AMC Ballistics Missiles Center, both of which decentralized weapon systems management and central buying functions, left Headquarters better able to handle the surveillance of worldwide procurement and production activities.

Proof of my sincerity in decentralization was demonstrated when the Air Staff, appreciating the way we were handling Logistics, turned Overseas Depots over to our control. We ran Japan, the Philippines, and Hawaii for a year. Then, because the Berlin airlift was so efficient, we turned them back to the Theatre Commanders.

Proof of my understanding of the significance of such decentralization would be demonstrated later in my General Mills activities.

Does significance lie in "firsts?" Then credit the fledgling Air Force with the first Comptroller organization, first Pentagon computer, and the first cost accounting system.

Does significance lie in how well you bring out the best in others? Then consider the day General Russ Dougherty, pilot and attorney, took advantage of my open-door policy and walked into my office almost in tears. He had been removed from flying status. I told him I would check on it, as this did not make sense to me. The Air Force was looking for pilots. I called General Kuter, head of personnel. He agreed. In a week the order was rescinded. Russ Dougherty went on to become Commanding General of the Strategic Air Command.

* * * *

Significance is often created by pomp and circumstance like the show we put on for Her Excellency Madam Vijayalakshima Pandit, High Commissioner for India to the United Kingdom. One such event was my own inspection visit in 1955, to our depots in France.

A red carpet and a camel were waiting for me at the airport. That camel was vicious. It whinnied, kicked, and spat. But the personnel at the base were also dangerous: we had to take special precautions to avoid being robbed. However, after the inspections were completed, two of the consultants with me arranged an invitation to a party at the home of the Duke and Duchess of Windsor. I was so glad that Pete had come along on this trip. We both enjoyed the Duke and Duchess. We also met and had a long talk with that noted Washington hostess, Pearl Mesta.

Speaking of parties, my last weeks in Dayton, where in several installments I had spent some seventeen of thirty years in the service, became a parade of cocktail parties, receptions, and banquets in my honor. My lifestyle has not been that of a party-goer, but I certainly received practice at it from Christmas 1958, to the date of my retirement, February 28, 1959. One of the youngest generals ever to receive a fourth star (I was 49) was now leaving the service of his country — the official service, at least. My retirement reduced the Air Force's four-star complement to ten.

I resolved to remain in the Air Force, in spirit. I had too many close ties to muster out. There were people I would never forget and institutions that I had helped to sire that I could never disown.

A Military Career Ends

And there was my staff. Mutual sorrow prevailed in my parting. I wrote them a memo which was later published in the magazine *AMC Worldwide*. I quote it now to end this chapter in my life:

"Goodbye is as hard to say as any word in the language. This is especially true when you must say it to the people who have contributed to whatever accomplishments you have achieved."

"As many of you know, I am retiring from active service on February 28. I have spent more than 30 years in the Air Force, 14 of them in the Air Materiel Command, and the last 7½ as AMC's commander.

"These have been eventful years, packed with the accelerating technology of a dawning space age, strained by the desperate tensions of two wars, and of a longer and, in some ways, more dangerous cold war.

"Yet these also have been gratifying years. You have made them so. On your loyalty, dedication, and hard work we have built a valid response to the challenges we face. We have gotten on with a difficult job.

"The task, of course, is unfinished. Much remains to be done. A significant part of the nation's security, its meaning of survival, its hope for a calmer, brighter future is in your hands. I hope to contribute too, but in a new way.

"My prayers will be with you, along with a gratitude deeper and more lasting than I can express.

"I am confident that my successor will enjoy the same loyalty and spirit of cooperation that you have shown me these past several years, and that each of you will continue to play a vital role in defense of the free world."

It is difficult to look back at one's own accomplishments and sort them out. So let me quote Missouri Senator Symington addressing the Senate on my retirement as printed in the March 5, 1959, issue of the Congressional Record:

"It is appropriate at this time to mention a few of the major contributions of this fine officer — contributions not only to the Air Force, but to the Department of Defense and to America.

In 1951, a Special Weapons Office was set up in Headquarters Air Materiel Command to centralize the command's participation in the atomic energy program.

In 1952, Air Materiel Command started to decentralize as a solution to the management problems of bigness. Workloads were broken down into more manageable segments and top management was left with more freedom to do its overall job of managing. In addition, actions were taken to reduce pipeline time lags and to standardize logistics for oversea operations. As an example, aerial resupply alone cut pipeline time for filling requisitions and reduced inventory levels by millions of dollars.

In 1953 a new technique, that of monetary inventory accounting, was tested in the Air Materiel Command, with the result that the system was adopted throughout the whole Air Force.

In 1954 Air Materiel Command installed electronic data processing equipment which translated the voluminous detail of logistics into more manageable terms and made possible logistics operations of unprecedented speed and flexibility.

In 1955 a worldwide transceiver network was installed to speed up the distribution of supplies needed by units of the Air Force wherever they might be.

In 1956 the Air Materiel Command Ballistic Missiles Office was set up — a milestone in logistics thinking and a prototype of a new era of space-age support.

In 1957 the logistics program was further streamlined so that much of our oversea military operations could be supported directly from this country — thereby reducing substantially the size and expense of our oversea logistic establishments.

In 1958 the Air Materiel Command Aeronautical Systems Center and the Air Materiel Command Ballistic Missiles Center were established to decentralize weapon system management and central buying functions.

This, then, is but a brief chronology of a few of the major contributions which General Rawlings has made to defense efficiency in recent years.

A Military Career Ends

As one who has worked with General Rawlings, I am proud to say, from personal knowledge, that his is a record of brilliance and of devotion to duty that should be imitated but would be difficult to equal."

PART III

Chapter IX

A General to General Mills

The review parade was over and the ceremony began. Because it was a rainy, blustery day, it had been moved indoors.

The huge Patterson Field hangar — nearly an acre of enclosed space — echoed to the sound of rolling drums. For the last time, eight base organizations were being presented to me. The date was Saturday, February 28, 1959.

"The 56th Fighter-Interceptor squadron, all present and accounted for, sir."

"Wright Air Development Center, all present and accounted for, sir."

"The Air Force Institute of Technology, all present and accounted for, sir."

Besides the eight base organizations also present and accounted for were twenty-two Air Materiel Command commanders who had flown in for my retirement ceremony from their areas and depots throughout the world. They were in two ranks a few feet from me.

I stood at attention.

Up until this moment, my retirement and my appointment to General Mills had been, in a sense, just another logistics maneuver. This had to be done. That had to be done. An objective had to be reached.

Now it was happening. It was subjective. I was the event. It

A General to General Mills

was impossible not to feel the emotional impact. I felt it deeply.

Beside me, also at attention, were General Thomas D. White, Air Force Chief of Staff, and my Vice Commander, Lt. General William F. McKee. Civilians, guests, and visiting military were seated in an audience half-hidden by red, white, and blue banners. In that audience were my wife, Pete, my oldest son, Peter, 27, my two middle sons, Gerry and Dick, and my youngest son, John, 17. On catwalks near the ceiling, youngsters crowded for a better look.

The drums rolled. I walked out a few feet, made an about-face, and saluted. The 661st all-brass Air Force Band played "The Star Spangled Banner."

General White approached me. I presented the command to him. He in turn presented it to General McKee who would hold it temporarily until the new Commander, Lt. General Samuel Anderson, could arrive and assume it.

General White turned back to me. He presented me with a retirement certificate and then pinned an Oak Leaf Cluster to the Distinguished Service Medal which I received at this very base in November, 1946, for my service in World War II. The Cluster is like a repetition of the Medal award. I listened as he read the citation.

"...distinguished himself by exceptional meritorious service...outstanding achievements, dynamic leadership...development of an air logistics system specifically tailored to the global requirements of the Air Force...

My mind wandered back over my life from Dayton's Department Store to Dayton, Ohio. Although I had clocked some 10,000 piloting hours in the air, my experiences were in business. From pots and pans to PX's and then to the largest business in the world: The Air Materiel Command. It had 197,000 employees around the world, and in my eight years had averaged over $10 billion a year in expenditures. I was leaving this for an organization with 13,500 employees that had grossed a half billion dollars the previous year. Was I doing the right thing?

The Band played "The Air Force March." The ceremony was over. I was a civilian.

I got into the official car that had been assigned to me and took my last ride, to my quarters. I inspected the house to make sure everything was moved out and that we were leaving the place clean.

We loaded up to go. It was noon when I got behind the wheel of my Cadillac, wearing the comfortable slacks and windbreaker that I wore whenever I went hunting. I sported a jaunty hat with a feather.

I drove off, waving to the last of the well-wishers. I was driving back to the state where I was born.

"Will you miss the art club, Pete?"

She had been given a farewell certificate just a few days before at a luncheon of the Brush and Palette art study group at the air base. It was signed by all the members.

"Ed, I'm sure art is alive and well in Minneapolis."

We discussed the ceremony and the people there. But my thoughts were of the future.

I went over and over in my mind the way Charles Bell had described General Mills activities, the financial situation, and the responsibilities he wanted me to assume. It was when we were both in Washington for an Air Force Association convention that he had made his pitch and I had made my decision.

"You will be doing the same work at General Mills, Ed," he had assured me.

"Spell it out," I insisted.

"Reducing costs, improving efficiency, enlarging profits."

"Wait a minute, Charlie," I interrupted, "we don't make profits in the Air Force."

"In a way you do. Just substitute stockholders for taxpayers."

"You're a fraction of the size of the Air Force," I baited him.

"But we're just as worldwide and diversified. We need a man with exactly your experience. You'll fit right in, Ed. Your official title will be financial vice president. You'll supervise activities of the comptroller's, treasurer's, and commercial development departments."

"The remuneration, Charlie. Is that also a fraction of the Air Force?"

He laughed. "Yes, Ed, but a fraction with a bigger numerator than denominator." It was my turn to laugh. He went on to explain stock options I would have. That really made the deal a financial step forward.

"You know, Charlie, it's not just the money. I've received some really sweet offers from big companies in recent months. I'm concerned about working for any company that I did business with for

A General to General Mills

the Air Force. Any such conflict of interest, no matter how slight, could be blown out of all proportion for me. So I have to be extra careful!"

"We have a mechanical division, Ed," he reminded me. "We are involved in search and track systems, guidance and navigations systems, underwater ordnance weapons, missile subsystems."

"I don't remember signing any contracts for the Navy," I replied.

I trusted Charlie and Charlie trusted me. We had worked together in the Air Force during the war and had a mutual respect. One way Charles Bell did not trust me was that I might take another offer. That's why he was putting on the pressure that day — a year before my retirement.

In a few minutes we were shaking hands on the deal.

So my conscience was clear on that score. My conscience was clear also on my ability to handle the job. I had not misrepresented myself in the least. I was exactly who my reputation claimed me to be. I knew what had to be done in business, by business, and for business. Plus I had proven I was blessed with the skill to do it.

Still, I knew the going would not be easy. Yes, I was returning to my native state, but I would be entering an environment foreign to me and having to speak a language new to me. Riding in the car, I began to think of the things I could do to meet the people with whom I would be working in an accelerated and more intimate way. Getting to know the food industry lingo would then come about as a natural result of that interaction.

We reached Chicago by late afternoon, found a suitable motel, and retired early. Quite early the next morning, we struck out for Minneapolis, some 500 miles away. By taking turns at driving, the two cars reached that city in late afternoon. We located the Bell Motel on Highway 12 not far from Minnetonka Mills where we had rented a house, with the help of retired Air Force Officers Chuck Kelly, a Prudential insurance agent and an old friend, whose son served on my AMC legal staff.

When we reached Minneapolis we drove to the house. It was a large, rustic, split-level surrounded by three acres of oak trees. Waiting for us was Chris Nelson, Purchasing Agent for General Mills. He had brought kindling and logs and had a roaring blaze going in the livingroom fireplace. I realized then that I would have no trouble getting to know such fine, thoughtful people.

The next day I reported to General Mills and was officially placed on their payroll. The first order of business was to meet the people with whom I would be having daily contact. Charlie Bell started this process himself and pretty soon it went along on its own momentum. Everybody was cordial and cooperative. I was briefed on many aspects of this huge company's far-flung operations.

Some press clippings were passed to me. Apparently the press considered my retirement and new appointment rather newsworthy. The Dayton *Daily News* headlined one story, "Rawlings Closes 30-Year Career." It covered the Wright Field ceremony and printed the whole citation accompanying the Oak Cluster award. An adjacent second story was captioned "General Joins Food Firm." It told of Charles Bell's announcement, as President, that I would be joining General Mills as vice president, that I would be serving on the executive council, and that I was also elected to the firm's Board of Directors.

The *New York Times* played it straight with a two column, top of the page, picture story in its Sunday, March 1, financial section. But then it referred back to how my employer in Minneapolis thirty years ago had tried to dissuade me from quitting my job to enlist in the Army Air Corps, saying that there was no money in aviation. The story suggested that I was now taking that advice.

Of the many clippings that were called to my attention, the story that the *Dayton Journal Herald* ran was unique. They had gone to the trouble of asking the top Air Force commanding generals to recall "what I always will remember about General Rawlings." These were printed on the front page under the photographs of the generals, eight in all.

When I saw this layout and recognized these eight officers, I suspected possible skulduggery, humorous putdowns, or digs. But as I read them, my heart went out to these great men for their generous appraisal of me and my work.

General Thomas D. White, Chief of Staff, who took part in the Dayton ceremony a few days before, said he remembered me best for "the unfailing courtesy and consideration extended to others whatever their position or rank might be."

General Curtis E. LeMay, then Vice Chief of Staff, USAF, recalled my "untiring efforts in helping build the Strategic Air Com-

A General to General Mills

mand into a powerful and modern combat force." (Because I had the same large physical build as General LeMay, who was very serious most of the time, I was called "the smiling LeMay" on the Base).

General O.P. Wayland, Tactical Air Commander, paid my wife a compliment by saying, "My earlier appraisal of his good judgment was confirmed when he wooed and won the fair Muriel Peterson."

Lieutenant General William E. Hall, Continental Air Commander, called me an able administrator and logistic expert but then tempered that by recalling the Air Secretary's picnic in Quantico. "There he demonstrated another facet of his all-around by expertly riding a donkey."

General Thomas S. Power, Commander-in-Chief, Strategic Air Command, recalled the many times he and I had worked closely together and expressed his appreciation for my "contributions to the present state of Air Force preparedness."

Similarly generous remarks were made by Lieutenant Generals Samuel E. Anderson, William F. McKee (my Vice Commander), and Frederic H. Smith, Jr., the latter stating, "His thinking is the epitome of intellectual honesty."

Now, without an ounce of modesty, that's what I call good reporting. Little wonder that the *Dayton Journal Herald* was in its 152nd year at that time, and at this writing, is still going strong.

This press round-up would not be complete if I did not also quote New Hampshire Senator Bridges, in *The Congressional Record:* "Another indispensable asset to General Rawlings has been his unwavering integrity. During his tenure as commander of Air Materiel Command, he was directly responsible for the expenditure or obligation of public funds in excess of $85 billion. He performed this task of high responsibility to the best advantage of the Air Force and to the Nation. His own integrity has been an inspiration to the many military and civilian officials who have assisted him in his great and complex task."

In those first few days and weeks at General Mills, I studied balance sheets and profit and loss statements. I analyzed where the bulk of profits were coming from and where the firm was not getting its money's worth for the capital investment involved. Gradually the people came into focus, and I began to realize why President Charles Bell needed me.

Rawlings

The Board of Directors was dominated by members who had served the company for three decades, including Charlie Bells' father, who had created the company back in 1928. Also, top executives were reaching retirement age. Three executive vice presidents were in line for Charlie's presidency when he moved up to board chairman. One, who headed the large flour and feed divisions, was nearing retirement age. Another headed the consumer foods operation; he was the youngest of the three and had not yet made the Board of Directors. The third headed the mechanical division and appeared to be the most eligible prospect but for some reason the board felt he was not the right man to succeed Charlie.

At any rate, after evaluating internal prospects, the Board felt that injecting a fresh viewpoint was critical to future progress. They responded to Charlie's recommendations and turned to me despite the fact I was three years his senior.

The company was faced with two dilemmas. One, although sales were going up, the profit rate was going down. Secondly, flour and feed, which had been the thrust of General Mills over the years, were running into stormy weather. Flour had dropped from 74 percent of sales in 1938 to 43 percent in 1958. Feed had retreated from 19 to 13 percent.

I began to talk in terms of hundredweights and calories. I was learning their language. I also found that, just as in the military, people were the most important factor. The right people in the right places make things flow smoothly.

Bakery flour captured my attention at the outset as a possible culprit in the unhappy profit picture at General Mills. I resolved very early in my first year with the company to make a thorough study of that major portion of the business. Besides their very low profit margin, the mills required frequent modernization to stay competitive. The man I tapped to do the study was Hoot Gibson, an old friend and a former Air Force officer who was then with Stanford Research Institute, an arm, at that time, of Stanford University. He agreed to take on the project and immediately put a team to work.

Gold Medal was a brand name with one of the best reputations. Certainly it was one of the oldest surviving brand names at the time, having originated in 1888 because it won a gold medal at the Cincinnati Exposition. Just the name Gold Medal flour was an

A General to General Mills

asset of inestimable value, as was Betty Crocker.

General Mills had other brand name assets, like Cheerios and Wheaties, both of which became more common breakfasts to me now than they had been before.

I examined the company's communications. I would be relying on communications to implement directives and to obtain information, as well as to transport warm bodies to and from inspections and meetings expeditiously. General Mills, at that time, had manufacturing and processing operations in twenty-six states and four foreign countries, from Mexico to Pakistan.

In my initial communications with people, I had to be especially diplomatic. Here was a four-star general being placed in a high level of responsibility, a stranger to the firm. I was suspect to everybody. Each one thought I might be taking aim to shoot him down. Had Charlie Bell brought in a hatchet man to do his dirty work?

For months this suspicion lurked in the minds of employees, but when they began to see that my chats with them and my insatiable hunger to know about them personally and the nature of their jobs was sincere, the imagined threats dissolved, and I began to get more cooperation and more effective relationships.

Another aspect of communications was travel. General Mills had two executive aircraft, World War II DC-3's. They were comfortable but exasperatingly slow. I thought a Lockheed Jet Star would do a better job, but in line with my "go slow" policy I asked the flight crew to look around to see what might be available. They came up with a recommendation that we buy a Lockheed Jet Star.

That plane worked out very well. Everybody was quite happy with it. I decided to dramatize the jet age in a way that might rev up some additional sales force enthusiasm. On the morning of a given day, I arranged with our sales people in New York, Chicago, and San Francisco to attend a sales breakfast with headquarters people.

We flew to New York and had our first sales breakfast. We took off for Chicago and conducted sales breakfast number two that same morning. We then departed for the West Coast and our third sales breakfast of the day. General Mills officials were quite pleased with the performance of their Jet Star.

Of course, I did not pilot these planes myself. I had logged 10,000 hours of piloting time out of Dayton, Honolulu, and Washington, but General Mills had their own flying crews, and I had no desire to create any tension with them.

Before a year was up, temptation was placed in front of me to fly again, The phone rang one morning with a call from a top executive of Trans World Airlines.

"General Rawlings, the rumor is out that you are not too happy with the food business."

"I don't know where you heard that," I replied, "but it is not true. I am enjoying my work with General Mills immensely."

"Be that as it may, General, I have been authorized to offer you the presidency of TWA."

"Well, I'm flattered." The words just hung there as my mind reeled with the impact of that offer. I had a chance to trade Wheaties for wings. It took me about a half second to decide. "TWA is a fine company, but I'm not available."

"Do you want time to consider, General Rawlings, and may we meet to discuss it?"

"It would be a waste of your time," I reaffirmed. "I'm looking forward to a challenging career with General Mills. I hope you find the right man."

When I hung up the phone, I did so with a sense of pride — not because of the prestigious offer just made to me, but because of my strength in resisting its attraction, a strength derived from a deep knowing that I had made the transition from the military to civilian life smoothly and successfully, and that General Mills was the right spot for me. I was ready to give it all I had.

It was great being back in Minnesota. It was my favorite hunting grounds because I knew it so well from my youth, and also because it was so close to Canada's geese country. Not only was our rented house in rural surroundings, but even the General Mills headquarters complex was twenty minutes outside of the city of Minneapolis and in a beautiful natural spot. The main building was modern in design with large glass areas that made the offices bright and provided them with views of the gardens, orchard, and pond.

The center section of the building was four stories high and was built around an atrium. Here an oriental garden complete with crane and pagoda accented the view. Offices were brightly carpeted and comfortably furnished. An executive dining room was available

A General to General Mills

to us, and I frequently enjoyed joining Charlie Bell there to touch bases. His interesting stories of past events at General Mills had a lot to do with making me feel part of the General Mills family.

I considered the library a fine feature of those offices. Just about everything that had ever been published on food and nutrition was included, from technical to popular.

As versed as I had been in military air materiel and its language, I now became fluent in the language of General Mills. I knew its product divisions forward and backward: the flour, feed, and specialty products division; the electronics group and chemical division; the grocery products division, the refrigerated foods division, and others. I could rattle off the Betty Crocker products, too — Betty Crocker's Orange Chiffon Cake Mix, Golden Pound Cake, Buttermilk Biscuits, Instant Mashed Potatoes, Pie Crust Mix, Safflower Oil, Good and Easy Cook Book, and many more.

I knew, too, that the formula for Bisquick had been created back in the early thirties. A Pullman cook developed the rough idea. He turned it over to a General Mills salesman riding on the train who, in turn, gave it to research man Charlie Kreff. It was tested and worked well. General Mills started making it in 1932.

Still, I made no major moves while serving on the Board of Directors. I listened and learned. Harry Bullis had resigned and been replaced by Gerald S. Kennedy as Chairman of the Board, about the time I joined the firm. Now, some two years later, Charles Bell moved from President to Chairman of the Board, and Kennedy stayed on as Chairman of the Board's Executive Committee.

That left the presidency open. Guess who was named to fill it? Yes, Ed Rawlings. Now I could no longer play a passive role. The General had become the General of General Mills.

Let me go back a spell in my private life. We lived in that rented house only about six months, because Pete was not happy in it. As those oak trees that surrounded it lost the few brown leaves that had hung on through the winter and its spring buds turned into spreading green leaves, the view became less and less, and pretty soon we were locked in by greenery. Pete felt restricted. She had been used to open views all of her life, starting with the beautiful mountain and sea vistas of Hawaii and continuing with the more open spaces of Virginia and Ohio. Now she was on the verge of claustrophobia.

Rawlings

That Labor Day weekend we took a house-hunting drive. We both liked the Lake Minnetonka area, so I headed there. We saw a few "For Sale" signs but not exactly what we were looking for. Then we saw a house right on the lake and a man adjusting a "For Sale" sign that he had apparently just finished installing.

"Can we look at this house?" I asked.

"I'm not the owner, I'm the agent," he replied. "I'll have to check with the owner."

"We'll wait," I said.

In a few minutes, he came back. "Park your car over there."

The grounds were beautiful, the lake exquisite, the house admirable — just what we both wanted. We were introduced to the owner, a doctor with the Veterans Hospital.

"You're lucky," he said. "I just put this house on the market today."

We talked price — and bought it. We lived happily in it for many years.

Part of my orientation at General Mills was to become active in local groups and organizations. It was a different situation than in Dayton where community relations were focused on lessening the negative impact of an air base on residential community. Here in Minneapolis there was no such negative factor at work. General Mills was a good neighbor, so the community relations thrust was to make it an even better neighbor.

One of the organizations I joined was the Minneapolis Chamber of Commerce, to which I was named General Mills delegate. The Minneapolis Chamber's main problem at that time was the St. Paul Chamber of Commerce. The two groups vied with each other to attract new companies, visitors, and conventions to their half of the Twin Cities.

Since it was my policy to listen until I was thoroughly versed in a problem area, I sat for hours at these Minneapolis Chamber meetings listening to members bemoaning the St. Paul competition and suggesting ways to counteract it.

To me, the answer was so simple. Still, I hesitated to voice it. Minneapolis was wasting promotional dollars fighting St. Paul and St. Paul was in turn wasting their promotional dollars fighting Minneapolis. Finally, in the middle of one of these nonproductive meet-

A General to General Mills

ings, I asked for the floor, and was recognized.

"Gentlemen," I said, "this is a no-win war for both sides. Why fight it? Both Minneapolis and St. Paul can make themselves the greatest attraction in the Midwest if they work together. Why not combine the two Chambers and form the Twin Cities Chamber of Commerce?"

I sat down. There was absolute silence. I looked at the faces around me. Eyes were diverted from me. I had really laid an egg. Somebody changed the subject. And that was the end of that.

...Until twenty years later. I received a letter from the Chamber president saying that a Twin Cities Chamber of Commerce was being formed. Some ideas take a long while to hatch.

I was hatching one at General Mills. Hoot Gibson had completed his study on the worldwide flour situation. It confirmed my own initial appraisal: a satisfactory return on flour mills was next to impossible. Translated into action, that meant: sell them.

They were the heart and soul of General Mills. They were what everybody had worked for since the company's start. Who was I — an outsider — to say get rid of them? If I made that proposal at a Board of Directors meeting, the silence would make the Chamber's silence sound like a jet roar.

But I was now President of the General Mills Board. The battle had to be joined.

Chapter X

Improving Profits

The fishing was slow that morning at 6:30 a.m. After casting on the shore of Lake Minnetonka for an hour, I had caught nothing. Ordinarily I would have a bass or two by this time. At least it gave me time to think.

I had put down roots in Minneapolis. In the five years I had lived there, I had joined the Minneapolis Club, Marsh Lake Hunting Club in Chaska, The Hazeltine National Golf Club, and the Wayzata Country Club. I served on a number of boards including the Northwest Bancorporation, the North Star Research and Development Institute, the Boys & Girls Club of Minneapolis, and the Greater Minneapolis Chamber of Commerce.

I was serving on a number of educational institution boards such as Hamline University, my alma mater; Mills College in Oakland, California, my wife's alma mater; Dunwoody Institute in Minneapolis; and the Minnesota State Junior College System. I had received honorary degrees such as Doctor of Business Administration from Hamline, Hendrix, and Tufts; and Doctor of Laws from the University of Dayton, Miami, and Ohio Wesleyan.

I was in my early sixties. Pete and I were in the prime of our marriage. I enjoyed her activities and she enjoyed mine. Family reunions with our four sons now included five grandchildren.

Was that a bite? I tugged on the line. False alarm. I decided

Improving Profits

to call it quits for the day, have breakfast, and go to work. I was no longer the baby of General Mills. General Mills, I felt, was my baby. And there was a lot of work to do.

I had the opportunity to test my muscle at General Mills in 1963. One of our lines was animal feed, mostly for turkeys. But the line itself was becoming a turkey. Despite the fact that feed formulations and feed management ideas were tested at the research farm near Indianola, Iowa, to determine the best and most economical method of poultry feeding; and despite the many textures and medications (a feed for every need), the feed business was in deep trouble.

So little capital was needed to get into the business of raising turkeys, for instance, that there was an over-supply of the birds. This meant that, come Thanksgiving or other holidays, the flood of turkeys sent to the market would drop the price below cost and the farmers could not pay their bills, including our feed bill.

We had no choice but to sell feed on credit. We accepted the turkeys as collateral. We found ourselves in the banking business with huge accounts receivable. Then when we got paid in turkeys instead of money, as was the case when low prices forced the farmers out of business, we found ourselves in the turkey business to boot. Often the farmers lost their turkey crop to disease or weather. Then we had no money and no collateral.

As a turkey farmer, General Mills had their same problems. Forced into the turkey business by reneging farmers, we owned tens of thousands of turkeys at one time. I remember one hot spell in California, we lost 5,000 turkeys in one day. I acted quickly.

After analyzing the Feed Department operating statements, I made a presentation to the Board of Directors.

"Gentlemen, recently 5,000 turkeys died from the heat in California on one day. *Our* turkeys. A total loss to us. I don't think our stockholders want to be in the turkey business. Please take a look at the figures I have passed around."

The directors looked at the Feed Department summary sheets.
"Any comments?" I asked.

There were some "pretty bads" and "not goods" and shaking of heads. I figured the time was right for a vote.

"All those in favor of dismantling and discontinuing the feed operation please so indicate."

It was unanimous.

A key man in the Feed Department was Gene Wolley. I put him in charge of the liquidation, sharing with him the principles I had help set up in dismantling war production out of Dayton. He did an outstanding job, recouping capital we could then put to work in the consumer businesses we knew best. As fast as we divested ourselves of losing feed operations, we found profitable new acquisitions.

Of course, I was pleased with the result. It brought real changes to the profit and loss statement. But what pleased me most was that unanimous vote. I had worked hard to win the confidence of my fellow board members. They had shown that confidence.

The outside man had become an inside man. It was time to take a bolder step.

I went up to Canada on a hunting trip. That wasn't the bold step, but it gave me time to do some thinking. I did not have to go to Canada. Minnesota always had birds galore, partly because the state ran a bird planting program. I was after ducks this day. Minnesota's ducks are plentiful, too, depending on the amount of fall rain. When the fall rain is heavy, potholes, particularly those in corn fields, become attractive to mallards. My father would shoot twenty five on days when the threshing crews were out working.

Canadian geese gather in the Hudson Bay area before migrating season to fatten up on blueberries. That was target on this trip. And I hit it again and again.

I also hit another target. I returned with my strategy set to turn around the descending profit curve at General Mills and to launch it upwards.

The national picture was this. General Eisenhower had vacated the White House in 1961. This elderly and staid Republican was replaced by a young and energetic Democrat, John Kennedy, who proclaimed what he called a New Frontier. These became the years of the Minimum Wage Act, the Peace Corps, and slum clearance. A trade expansion act, passed in 1962, gave the United States more flexibility in dealing with Europe's Common Market. Inflation was a

Improving Profits

problem. When steel companies increased the price of steel in April, 1962, despite their tacit agreement not to, Kennedy diverted government contracts to other steel mills and thus compelled the United States Steel Corporation and others to cancel the increase.

Our flour mills were caught between unreduceable costs and unraisable prices. As to prospects for the future, I had Stanford Research Institute's dismal outlook, an irrefutable report by one of our country's most prestigious research organizations.

I had three smart, hard-working young men on my staff: Louis "Bo" Polk, Jim Summer and Dick Schall. They seemed just the right ones for my next step. I called them in to my office one morning. Polk had been vice president of Sheffield Corporation; Summer was a West Pointer, with a masters degree in mathematics from Michigan University, who had been doing research for AVCO; Schall was one of our more promising young executives.

"Look over this report, fellows." I handed each a copy of the SRI report. "Take your time." I sat back at my desk and watched them. As they scanned the pages, I heard an occasional "damn," "wow," and "ouch."

When they had gotten the drift, I interrupted them. "What do I do about this report?"

Bo Polk spoke up first. "General, we have to examine this in the light of how it affects planning here at General Mills."

The other two nodded agreement.

"Good idea, Bo. Let's do it. Can you fellows handle it?" All three replied affirmatively. "Same time, same day next week?" I asked in a way that commanded a yes answer. I got it.

I kept busy that week inspecting some of our far-flung facilities. The inspections were a regular part of my activities pretty much as they had been in the Air Force.
Sometimes a few members of the Board came along. It could be the Angle Food line at Rexdale, Ontario; or a company subsidiary cereal packaging line in Bromborough, England; or the Bellera mill in Buffalo. There were scores of installations that could always benefit from the shoring up that a personal visit by General Mills's "top brass" induced. People like to know you care about them.

Inspections are less a matter of looking for trouble, rarely did they ever uncover any deviate operations, and more a matter of supporting the people who work for you. People respond to your interest.

Conferences and sales meetings were another source of travel. A typical example of such an event was, say, the Chemical Division's Annual Sales Roundup. One year it was held at the Wagon Wheel Inn at Rockton, Illinois. I would give the kick-off talk on opening day. If other Board members came along, they too would give talks throughout the program. Officers of the Chemical Division would make presentations on critical aspects of the Division's activities, such as research, marketing, and advertising.

It was common for discussion groups to be organized to renew the ideas presented at these earlier sessions. If my schedule permitted, I enjoyed wandering in and out of these discussion groups to listen to concerns and the creative ideas to solve them. If some comment struck me as particularly pertinent, I would find out the name of the employee and note it down for possible future reference.

People in a company are its most important assets. You don't see them on a balance sheet or on a profit-and-loss statement. Still, they make the difference. They make a bigger difference if you treat them right. This does not always mean more money. Right treatment means recognition, consideration of feelings, proper working conditions, and excitement on the job.

The latter is especially important where sales are involved. Selling can become humdrum without an occasional change of pace. The definition of humdrum might be "without excitement," and this leads to a lack of enthusiasm.

At the Chemical Division's Sales Meeting I just described, the agenda included an annual golf tournament and the presentation of awards for meeting or beating quotas. We encouraged such events as recipe contests, visits by celebrities, and prizes for creative suggestions. At any one time you might find anything from an art exhibit to a beard-growing contest.

Those were internal activities, as opposed to the public activities we generated in order to whip up consumer interest and enthusiasm. These were on a national and international scale, involving motion picture and television stars, interwoven with our advertising and publicity, so as to add value to another non-measurable asset — our brand names. More about this type of excitement later.

My three-member team showed up on schedule with the flour

Improving Profits

summary I requested. Bo Polk spoke up first, followed by Jim Summer and Dick Schall.

Said Bo, "We have 17 mills. We are the biggest in the world. But we are paying for the privilege."

Jim echoed that, adding, "Divestiture can lead to tax problems, but we've found a way to minimize that."

Dick offered, "We should stay in the home flour business, as it is more profitable."

We kicked around a lot of points in that meeting. It boiled down to my preparing a proposal for action based on their recommendations and my own contributions, all supported by the SRI original report.

I thanked the team. "You fellows are not off the hook yet. I still need your help. I'll give you a call when I've worked up the proposal." I already had a hunch of how I was going to need them, but first I had to do my homework.

How do you tell a mother to divest herself of her child? That was, in effect, what I was about to ask General Mills to do, the people who created the company. I was about to ask those people to divest themselves of their creation.

In 1888, James S. Bell had moved from Philadelphia to Minneapolis to head up the Washburn Milling Company, predecessor of the Washburn-Crosby Company, which had a number of flour mills, strategically situated between wheat growers and city wheat eaters. In 1928 his son, James Ford Bell, merged Washburn-Crosby Company with a number of regional milling companies to form General Mills, a national organization.

Jim Bell also launched Betty Crocker and Wheaties. He poured money into research and created a food processing giant. Charles H. Bell was the eleventh generation Bell in the milling business. Although he became President in 1952, his father still remained on the Board, heading up two powerful Board committees, technological progress and finance. Charlie's father was still on the Board when I arrived and remained almost up until the time of his death in 1961, at the age of 81.

In the years just before and just after my arrival, Charlie had seen the diversification effort go sour with the sell-off of the electric appliance division and the lack of progress in the mechanics division. This served to reinforce the "I told you so" attitude of old-time General Mills executives, many of whom had served the Company for three decades and were nearing the retirement age. The makeup of the Board reflected this same conservatism and intransigence.

I would need to educate each Board member before the meeting at which I would make my divestiture proposal. For such a proposal to come from the Company President could be considered suspect. Here is where I saw how my three-man team could assist. I would tackle the Board Chairman myself.

I could be up against a problem with Charlie that went beyond the tendency to protect what he'd built. Charlie was a strong advocate of bigness. I could hear Charlie's voice in the Company film he narrated, entitled "Our Challenging Future."

"What duties do we of General Mills owe ourselves and the world in our unfolding future?" he asks. "We must do a bigger job each year than ever before, beginning right now!"

Well, beginning right now, I had to ask the man who spoke these words to agree to do a smaller job. It loomed as a big job for me.

We had lunch. We discussed my conclusions and recommendations at great length. Charlie was completely supportive. It was that easy. He was on my side.

I then asked Charlie to help sell the program first to his brother, a large stockholder and head of the Red Owl grocery chain, a man we could not afford to alienate. Then he would approach several other key personnel in General Mills.

At lunch a few days later he assured me, "It looks like clean sailing."

My presentation outline to the Board was now completed, but my strategy was not to present the proposal cold at a meeting. I called back my three young friends.

"My presentation is complete." I passed it around to them and explained it just the way I would to Board members. "Any questions?" There were none. "Any suggestions for improvement?" There were none.

"You have done an excellent piece of work on this matter, fellows. But there is one last step I want you to take." They all had a "what-else-could-there-be?" expression on their faces.

"I am going to assign several Board members to each of you.

Improving Profits

You will hand carry this proposal to them, explaining that it is my wish that they have a chance to study it before next week's meeting. You will explain what it covers, pretty much the way I just explained ti to you, answer questions if you can, and let me know that each mission has been accomplished."

To my knowledge, I was smashing protocol to smithereens. But the strong medicine I was prescribing seemed to require strong preliminary measures. My three-man team left on its mission, albeit in a daze at the innovative procedure I had thrust upon them. I did not sit back to await their reports. I still had to bone up on my figures and be prepard for any eventuality:

    1. Doesn't divestiture entail sacrifice of assets?
    2. Why not get rid of consumer flour, too? We could have a cleaner divestiture.
    3. What are we going to do with the capital we release, and how do we know we can get a better return than we are getting now?
    4. If acquisitions for diversification are planned, have we forgotten what happened to us in electrical appliances and electronics?

I could not prepare for every possible confrontation, but I could prepare for those I could dream up myself.

Time became a factor. I wished I had planned on a meeting the following month. All my commitments seemed to be converging on me. In addition, I now served on the Air Academy Board of Visitors, a Presidential appointment one dares not turn down. Incidentally, Senator Barry Goldwater was Chairman of that Board at the time I was appointed. We were both reappointed to another four-year term, so I had the privilege of getting to know the Senator over that eight-year period.

Not only did outside commitments impinge on my time, but now that I was fully responsible I was swamped with matters demanding attention.

I asked Hay and Associates, of Philadelphia, to do what they were expert at: set measures of executive performance. They had given us the guidelines we needed, and now we were in the midst of using them. Not as a bible, however. You can't be that rigid in dealing with people.

Rawlings

We had been making inadequate use of data processing. A first generation UNIVAC file computer was helpful in payroll and accounting. I wanted a total system. So we acquired a Honeywell 800 computer and housed it in a new $1.5 million Data and Communications Center next to our home office. Now it was being manned six days a week, 24 hours a day, doing filing, collating, storing, rearranging, sorting, processing, and printing.

In effect, it was handling all of our business — past, present, and projected — at speeds of a millionth of a second per entry. It gave me a total electronic data processing system for better control of advertising, product planning, 13,000 employees, inventory control, and day-to-day sales. To run this show, I had also "acquired" Louis "Bo" Polk, a young industrial engineer only four years out of Harvard Business School. Polk was an excellent addition to our staff. I had practically daily contact with him as my connection to all of this important data.

The open-door policy that I insisted on in Dayton, I had successfully used for a while at General Mills. But then, even though I got to my office at 7:30 each morning, the speed with which matters closed in on me in effect closed the door on others who wanted to see me. I mean it, I was busy.

Still, everything got done. The answers to those four possible questions? Of course...

> 1. The feed business liquidation cost us nothing. The poultry operations were well disposed of by Gene Woolley. The soybean operations also cost us nothing to dispose of. Sewell Andrews did an excellent job. To continue either of these operations would have really cost us money. Likewise, the General Mills Commodity business was successfully discontinued without sacrifice of assets.
> 2. No, we should keep the mills turning out flour for consumers. Bakers tell us what they will pay us for our flour. We tell consumers what they will pay us for our flour. Look at the difference that makes in terms of profit. We have nine mills, serving the bakers, barely on the profit side. We have eight mills making flour for consumer products showing a good

Improving Profits

profit, When we sell the nine mills, General Mills will no longer be the biggest in the business, but we'll eventually be able to show bigger profits.

3. We have been looking around for profitable acquisitions. You may hear more from me real soon on three companies: Monet Custom Jewelry, Eddie Bauer, and Talbots — all promising new possibilities for General Mills.

4. Mistakes have been made in acquisitions in the past. Today we have better electronic data processing for more efficient evaluation and control. We are also more flexible and decisive. If an acquisition does not pan out, we can sell it and take on another.

As I said, who could predict the direction a Board member might take in obstructing this monumental step? I could sit back in the chair behind my desk, smoking my pipe, thinking of possible questions and come up with a new challenge with every puff. To heck with it. Unless my three team members came back with a negative report, and I would handle such an eventuality with expediency if and when it arose, I would consider myself as prepared as I could be for the Board meeting.

One by one Polk, Summer, and Schall reported in after each Board member visit. No questions, No objections. Positive response. Agreement, no problem. I checked each name off on the list. Pretty soon all were accounted for. No objections were voiced. Now I was ready for the meeting.

The big day arrived. Board members took their seats. After the usual preliminaries, I brought up the flour mill problem and the proposed solution.

It passed unanimously!

I had lived with this problem for so long that it took some days to realize that it was no longer a problem matter but a plan of action matter. We had to close the mills. We had to attempt to relocate the people in other jobs where possible. We had to sell the machinery, equipment, and real estate.

I turned this task over to the manager of the Flour Division, Bill Humphrey, briefing him on property disposal practices that had worked so well in the Air Force. Bill Humphrey did a first class job.

General Mills took a mighty step forward. It was no longer

in the bakery flour business, but still milling flour for consumer products. Some twenty-five years later, this is still the policy, as profits have been rising steadily.

In 1959, sales were half a billion dollars. In 1986, they were ten times more: five billion dollars. In 1959, profits were nine million dollars. In 1986 they were $325 million, nearly forty times more.

As recently as early 1987, United and Babson's Reports, a financial news service out of Boston, said this about General Mills: "Having divested 26 marginal businesses, the firm, is clearly focused on packaged foods...For the current fiscal year, we look for net to rise 24 percent, with a similar gain expected in 1988. The stock is a buy for long-term growth." Apparently, the process of pruning we started a quarter century ago is on-going.

As soon as the bakeries heard about our divestment plan, they made a fuss. In no way did they want us to get out of the bakery flour business. Divestiture would probably lead to diversification in the ownership of those mills, and the bakers would lose the price control they enjoyed with us. That meant higher prices to them. Their objections in no way delayed our divesting of these nine mills. The remaining eight mills gave us ample protection in the family flour field, where good profits could be reaped. And we would be acquiring freed capital to invest in expanding the Gold Medal line and its markets.

To me, the most sensitive part of the liquidation of those nine mills was the people who worked there, over 1,000. I felt personally responsible for their welfare and made no secret of this to Bill Humphrey. Many of these workers were old-timers, eligible for retirement, so they did just that. A number of other able workers we could transfer to our other divisions, and still more were able to remain with the mills' new owners. All in all, very few were left without a job. Humphrey handled it beautifully.

Charlie Bell, the man who was most identified with the flour mills and who I had expected would put up the strongest fight to defend them, turned out to be my strongest supporter. He later explained the reason to me:

"Ed, I knew the picture. I understood what had to be done. But I could not bring myself to face it. I have been so close to the millers all of my working life that it would be like cutting off my own arm. It was psychologically impossible for me to do the job my-

Improving Profits

self." I nodded understandingly, and he continued, "You must give me credit for one thing though, Ed."

"What's that, Charlie?"

"I brought in the right man for that job."

I was now flying high. It had looked impossible to me, too. But I had moved step by step and won. I had the guts to follow through on my convictions. I had the data needed to support those convictions. I had knowledge to interpret data. And I had love and respect for people, which enabled me to use their talents, look out for their welfare, and be sensitive to their feelings.

I did not recognize it at the time, but the most significant effect of the bakery flour sell-off was what it did to the thinking of our key executives. In the new consumer business, the executive thought in terms of promotions and advertising, possibly in terms of several million dollars. This opened up new vistas of opportunity.

Back home that night, Pete had a crackling blaze going in the fireplace. I told her the good newes. We embraced. It was a relief for her, too, as she was with me every risky step of the way.

We sat down by the fire and I lit my pipe. We did not have to speak. Our togetherness spoke volumes. But this night there was a differnce. I felt like a new man.

I thought of the long effect this might have on General Mills's future policy.

Chapter XI

People Power

The machinery and equipment from a number of our closed mills was sold to other millers. A couple of mills were sold intact. Others that had fallen too far behind in modernization became victims of their own obsolescence and were razed. One of the mills sold intact was our latest mill called the Bellera. It brought a good price. Even where there were losses, the tax write-off made up for them, to a large degree. The whole divestiture process took about a year. All in all, divestiture's cost was minimal.

Money rolled in that we could use for capital reinvestment; that is, acquiring new machinery, new equipment, new ways of producing profit-making products.

There was another way to invest capital. You could invest it in your brand names, like Gold Medal or Wheaties. This meant more advertising, more publicity, and more public relations. These appear on financial statements as expenditures, not investments. Yet, they were indeed investments in the long run.

What the real impact of getting out of baking flour had on top management at General Mills was they began to think not just in terms of cents per hundredweight, but in broader terms of percentage profit.

I was now able to talk to top management about promoting consumer products. Whereas the idea of an extra million dollars in advertising was abhorrent to their old ways of thinking, now they

People Power

understood that extra advertising money brought a higher percentage of profit, and that was the bottom line.

The problem was to find nutritious food products that were attractive to the buying public. We could do this through our own research or acquisitions. I encouraged activity in both directions. As a result, in the ensuing years of my presidency a sizable number of additions were made to the company's breakfast cereal and dessert mix lines; a family of refrigerated foods was broadened; new special products were introduced for the hotel-restaurant-institution trade; and new chemical developments began to meet with success.

What a pleasure it was, being relieved of having to think in temrs of penny flour. It was literally a "penny ante" business. You watched every penny or you could lose your shirt. You had to compete with every little mill somebody started up. It was a restricting influence on our thinking.

Now our thinking was free. We broadened our horizons. As we left our penny flour behind, we could concentrate our thinking on more strategic issues like advertising, public relations, and promotion. We could turn our thoughts to consumer needs and how we could fill them.

These were the years that we got into the restaurant business, the clothing business, the catalog business, and others.

Acquisitions can turn out well or they can turn sour. Financial statements are your guiding light, but they often do not reflect inherent problems in the firm you acquire or the industry it is in. It is said everybody's grass looks greener than your own. An acquisition looks inviting, but once you have it, there's more crabgrass in its lawn than you expect.

New businesses have been acquired; then they have been spun off on their own, or sold. But General Mills consumer foods go on forever. At this writing, consumer foods have been at the core of General Mills business for forty years, albeit falling from 95 to 68 percent of total sales. Its five-year average return on identifiable assets was 28 percent in 1985, one of the highest in the food industry.

The second largest part of General Mills business in 1985 was the restaurant business started in my tenure as President and which grew steadily since then to become about one quarter of total sales. The decision which we made in the middle sixties to get into the restaurant business was based on projections we had that the eating-out habits of consumers was growing at a faster rate than the eating-at-home habit was. By being in both places, General Mills could not lose.

Part of this strategy was an increased emphasis on sales to hotels, restaurants, and institutions of food service products. We used flour to pilot General Mills to a bigger position in high-margin convenience foods.

Where I saw an existing line, such as instant mashed potatoes, faltering, we developed a new mashed potato product and, with strategic and tactical marketing, pushed it into first place.

In the late sixties we entered the $680 million market for salty snack foods. Conventional snacks were perishable; they had a shelf life of only three weeks. Our Buttons and Bows, Big G's, Daisy's, Bugles, and Whistles had a nine-month shelf life. This meant we could ship larger quantities — freight-car loads — at large distribution cost savings.

In 1966, we acquired the Tom Huston Peanut Company. Its sales were excellent. It may have been one of the reasons we looked into the leisure time field of products. After all, people ate peanuts during leisure time activities, and, with work hours shrinking, there was more time for television viewing, sports, travel, and just plain home recreation.

Our sortie into leisure activities netted us Rainbow Crafts with its popular Play-Doh (this "dough" was not made with flour); Craft Master Corporation, which pioneered the famous paint-by-numbers; toy-making Kenner Products; and the venerable Parker Brothers, founded in 1883, located in Salem, Massachusetts, the creators of the perennially popular game Monopoly. Leisure activities now became a separate division.

I was sitting at my desk in the executive wing one day contemplating what I could do to make General Mills products more readily recognizable by the public.

We had good brand names but no common "logo." There was a small "G" on all boxes and packages but it did not do the job. Why not a big "G"? I called in an excellent advertising agency and explained what I wanted.

They came back with more big "G"s than I knew existed —

People Power

script, Old English, block letters, etc. Finally, I settled on the Big "G" we have today.

I needed Charlie Bell's OK. But he was away on a cruise. Timing was important in adopting this logo uniformly on our packaging. So I placed a call to the cruise ship. It happened to be in a part of the world where the time was about 2 A.M. Charlie came to the phone expecting an emergency. The Big "G" understandably seemed out of context with his own points of reference, but he generously gave me his consent.

Ever since then the Big "G" has been on millions of packages doing its job. More and more people every day, when they hear or see the Big "G", think of General Mills.

One day I got a call from General White, Chief of Staff of the United States Air Force.

"I need your help, Ed," he said.

"Name it," I replied.

"As you may know, we have over a quarter million troops in Viet Nam. It's a major supply project. You established the logistics we're still using. We'd like you to take a look and see how they are working."

"Where do you want me to go?"

"Saigon."

Looking back now, I am surprised at how quickly I responded, "Sure!." It had taken me years to adjust to my new life as a business executive at General Mills. In an instant, I was ready to put my military cap back on.

"Who can I have on my team?" I asked.

"Whomever you want," General White replied. "When can you be ready to leave?"

"Just give me a few days," I said.

"I'll cut your temporary orders later today," he stated.

When I hung up, my head was reeling with all the arrangements I would have to make in a hurry. First, I had to decide whom I wanted on the team and get their okay.

The first man I contacted was General Wolfe, retired, who had been head of aircraft procurement. Next, I got "Dusty" Rivers, my old aide; and Gordon Reed, a businessman from Greenwich, Connecticut, with whom I had dealings when he headed the aluminum

Rawlings

and magnesium division of a large company in World War II.

We went to an Air Force base in San Francisco to see how materiel was being handled, then to Hickam Air Force Base in Honolulu, Guam, Clark in the Philippines, Taipei, Hong Kong, and on to Saigon. In other words, we checked out the supply lines from their point of origin in the United States to their point of use in Viet Nam, with an eye toward transit time, condition on arrival, and other factors influencing the efficient flow of materiel.

We did not go beyond the ports to the fighting areas, as that was under local commander control and beyond our Air Force logistical scope. But we still got a close-up view of wartime conditions.

I was completely satisfied with the smooth flow of materiels, as were the members of my team. It was particularly gratifying to see a system that I had set up years before, including the elimination of Pacific depots, now working efficiently years later when the chips were down.

There was a difference in age between top echelon military people and top echelon business people. I worked with relatively young senior officers in the Air Force. In its November 1, 1948, issue, *Life* magazine said, "These dashing young airmen, even at a desk, are serious far-sighted executives." The average age of Air Force generals was 47. At the top in 1948 was General Hoyt Sanford Vandenberg, only 49. General Muir S. Fairchild, Vice-Chief of Staff, was the oldest at 54. Lieutenant General Elwood R. Quesada, 44, was in charge of coordinating air support with ground troops and naval forces. Lieutenant General Curtis E. LeMay was the Air Staff's Strategic Boss at a young 41. As Air Comptroller, I was then 44, a Lieutenant General, and when I got my fourth star a few years later I was the youngest ever to make a full general in the Air Force.

At General Mills the equivalent of "senior officers" were the department heads and Board of Directors' members. Their average age was a good deal more than 47. I don't have the statistics, if indeed they exist, but just counting gray hairs, I would put the increment of age over the Air Force Generals' 47 at ten to fifteen years. It was the custom in large corporations for staff executives to retire at 65, Board members at 70.

Seldom do you see generals on active duty at such ages; their thirty years of service are usually over at an earlier age, as was mine.

People Power

But, is our country missing out on some expert leadership? Are retired senior officers truly ready for retirement? Or, should they be encouraged to share their expertise further into their so-called "golden years"?

And what about mandatory retirement for commercial and industrial leaders? Are we losing valuable brains there, too? I will have comments in Part IV, but meanwhile you can bet that my answer to that question is "yes."

The whole Viet Nam inspection trip took a bit over a week. It was an exhilarating experience. I immediately wrote my report to General White. It was positive all the way.

Overnight I was back to work on civilian problems at General Mills — the appointment of six new vice presidents from General Mills executives; the planning of a dinner for food editors at a conference in which we would show off some of our new food products; checking television shows for our possible sponsorship.

On the subject of television, we had an opportunity to sponsor Tennessee Ernie Ford doing a Christmas show. There was some feet dragging in the decision-making process, and I wound up with it on my desk, where the "buck" had a habit of stopping. It looked good to me. I was not too happy with the way General Mills was buying television time in those days. I felt we should be doing more important and worthwhile programming. Ford's "Story of Christmas" seemed a move in the right direction.

Since I was supposed to appear briefly on the show, I went to New York to meet Ford. We got along fine. The Christmas show turned out to be a public relations boost for General Mills. Although some of our marketing people were not ecstatic, the show got excellent ratings, and research indicated that the show had good commercial impact for General Mills. We repeated "The Story of Christmas" the followng year.

I kept up my friendship with Tennessee Ernie Ford. He was on the crew of the B-24 headed by Russ Dougherty which did yeoman work in World War II. So when the Air Force Association had their annual conclave in Washington, D.C., of which Dougherty was then president, Tennessee Ernie Ford was the emcee. He had been the bombardier. The rest of the crew was also there: the radio man, the engineer, the co-pilot. I enjoyed that meeting and got to know Ernie Ford through my military eyes.

Later, I took him hunting and fishing. We had a great time. To illustrate what a fine human being he is, years later when he was in Minneapolis for a show at the State Fair, he called me only to find out that I was in the hospital for surgery. He found the time to come over to the hospital to see me. All the nurses were wide-eyed. I'm sure their temperatures went up. When he left, I was surrounded.

"How do you know him?"

"Is he coming back?"

"What's he like?"

Hardly a year went by when I did not get together with Ernie Ford on a social basis. When I went to Hawaii some time after my retirement from General Mills, we met there, too, as Hawaii was one of his favorite places. A great friend of his was the late Earl Thacker, a big name in Hawaiian real estate. Ford gave Thacker a Palomino horse. Later Ford built himself a retreat in northern Idaho.

About another retreat, Wondra Island. When I first became aware of its availability, I was convinced it could be a boon to General Mills personnel as an executive vacation spot and conference center. There are very few places like it in America. Frank Tenny and I found it on one of our occasional fishing trips, this one was to Rainy Lake between Minnesota and Canada. We camped with an old Indian family, and Frank showed me an island near where his father had been bringing a Boy Scout Troop from Tulsa. I really liked it.

Wondra Island is located in Rainy Lake, just across the Canadian border from Minnesota. Its access from Minneapolis is by a 250 mile drive to International Falls and another few miles by boat or float plane.

I negotiated with the real estate firm that had the island listed for sale. Charlie Bell supported my proposal to buy it and to build suitable structures on it. The Board approved the purchase price plus $50,000, the estimated cost of a ranch-type cabin.

My friend Alton Raney gave me a set of plans for his duck camp in Stuttgart, Arkansas, that I found perfect. Our engineers estimated the cost to duplicate his building at under $50,000, my autho-

People Power
rized limit.

We got underway but, unfortunately, the cost headed higher and higher. It was going to be a good deal over the ceiling. We stopped work and I laid the problem in Charlie's lap. Once more he went to bat for me: the Board approved a higher sum. We were able to resume construction. He was mighty good at getting me off the hook.

Eventually we added two guest houses and a caretaker's house to its 37 acres. The latter had, in addition to an apartment, two bunk rooms. We built a pier suitable for boats and pontoon plane. Gasoline tanks, diesel tanks, and two diesel generators gave us the all-weather heat and power we needed. Later we had a sauna, a woodshed, and a fish-cleaning shed.

Rainy Lake is a sportsman's paradise — fishing, hunting, skeet shooting, hiking, swimming, boating. I had already hunted there and knew that the area had abundant duck, grouse, deer, and even bear.

Wondra Island became an executive seminar center, a sales incentive bonus, a strategy planning locale, a meeting facility, and last, but not least, a vacation retreat. Why should not General Mills people enjoy their leisure time also? Here were ideal facilities to get away from the cares of the world and enjoy outdoor living while still maintaining basic comforts. One might be right in calling it a luxury, but, if so, it was a luxury we had earned. Top executives had their own places. Now General Mills had a place where the medium income employee would not be saddled with expensive hotel rates.

If people are responsible for a company's success, as I firmly believe they are, then they need to be shown how well they are appreciated.

The opposite philosophy is more frequently encountered. Management seeks to fix the blame for mistakes rather than to reward success. So they weed out those people and wind up with blameless personnel who are useless as far as real progress is concerned because they are brainwashed out of taking risks.

It is the boldness, the freshness, and the daring of new ideas that create progress. It is more conducive to continued progress to reward success than it is to punish the inevitable attempts that do not pan out.

It was the General Mills policy long before I arrived to encourage good performance. They certainly practiced it on me. A year

Rawlings

after I joined the company as financial vice president, I was also named executive vice president in charge of the consumer food division. Eight months later, on the resignation of the vice president in charge of mechanical, chemical, and research projects, this division was also placed under my supervision.

A few months after that, in June 1961, I was named by President Charles Bell to be executive vice president for operations and finance, responsible directly to the President. Now I was in charge of operating the chemical, feed, flour, grocery products, refrigerated foods, and specialty products divisions as well as the Electronics Group, Sperry (West Coats), and General Mills Limited of England.

That was also the year I was moved up to company President (December 1961) with Charlie Bell becoming Chairman of the Board.

On November 6, 1967, I was elected Chairman of the Board while still continuing as Chief Executive Officer; Charlie Bell remained on the Board as chairman of its Executive Committee and head of both the Finance and the Research Policy Committees.

I was 63, I could remain Chief Executive Officer for only two more years and on the Board for ten more years. I had a "love affair" with General Mills. It was mutual. I appreciated them and showed it in every way I could. They appreciated me and showed it in every way they could.

I wrote a brief statement for our magazine *The Modern Millwheel* on the occasion of my becoming Chairman of the Board:

"I welcome the opportunity to serve the company in this new capacity and know that all of you will give our new President, James P. McFarland, the same support you have given me. I am delighted that Mr. Bell is remaining active in the company, and I am looking forward to working with him, Jim McFarland, and all of you in building an even greater company."

Jim McFarland, 55, had been serving as Executive Vice President of the company for several years. In fact, he had spent his entire business life in General Mills. He received his B.A. from Dartmouth and his MCS in 1934 at the Amos Tuck School of Business Administration. Then he went right to work for the company in grain accounting at our Wichita, Kansas, plant. We had a good relationship, seeing eye to eye in most matters.

I must admit to another "love affair" — this one with a wom-

People Power

an. Her name was Betty Crocker. My wife was not jealous because she is an imaginary woman. Still, she was one whom we at General Mills could not help but think of as real. Over the years there have been hundreds of fellows who have proposed marriage to her. Can you imagine their hurt when they were informed that Betty Crocker was only an artist's drawing?

Her persona was created in 1921 as a pen name for the young man whose job it was to answer consumer inquiries for the then Washburn Crosby Company. He felt that the housewives who wrote him would have more confidence if the answer came from a woman. The name Crocker was selected to honor a retired executive of that company and the name Betty selected because of its warm and friendly sound.

For years Betty Crocker remained just that, a signature on letters. Then she became a voice on radio, a daytime food service program. It was not until 1936 that she became visible. An artist painted a face that was a blend of the features of women working in the Home Service Department. This same face was redrawn in 1955, giving Betty a smile and a more mature look.

After my joining General Mills, and during my tenure, Betty Crocker received three face-lifts. After all, she was appearing on flour mixes, recipe books, and products used by millions. She had to reflect the times. The first of these three artistic revisions was in 1965. Our goal was to enhance Betty's prestige with a new generation of homemakers. In 1968 the second revision made Betty more ladylike and sophisticated. Then in 1972 we had Betty Crocker go more casual, with a shorter and wavier hairdo.

We all loved Betty Crocker. After all, she was the source of easy-to-do, tasty, nutritious foods, and is not that the way to a man's heart? Today, despite her 66 years, Betty Crocker looks 36 and could pass as the daughter of her forerunners. The Betty Crocker Food and Publication Center conducts regular market surveys of the acceptability of new products. As to the updated symbol of those products, women young and old have described their perception of Betty Crocker as "friendly," "intelligent," and possessing "leadership qualities." Now who could not love a woman like that, especially when she turns in such good profit statements year after year?

The greatest event in the lives of everybody at General Mills was the Annual Betty Crocker search for "The American Homemaker of Tomorrow." Every school, public, private, or parochial, was invited to compete. The winner received a $5,000 scholarship to the college of her choice and the course of her choice. Many thousands of schools participated, and hundreds of thousands of applicants. You can't buy that kind of publicity.

At best, investing advertising money into brand names is an iffy business. No data processing system can give you short-term answers. How much on newspaper space? How much on television or radio? What magazines? You have to use gut feeling. It's like flying blind without instruments. Intuitively you do what seems to be called for. Now, as to long-term answers, that's different. You can see the trends and the results. Your data processing system gives you bird's-eye views that are of inestimable value in making broad policy decisions. In the case of Betty Crocker, that name was so dependable that we knew whatever we put into it we would get back, and then some.

Another area where you could not depend solely on data processing was in acquisitions. Some of our best "buys" were made on the kind of "data" you could not process. Take Eddie Bauer.

Somebody once gave me a hunting jacket. I had never seen one quite like it. The people who made it were obviously hunters. The pockets were in the right places; it was warm and yet lightweight; it could stand abuse. I looked at the label — Eddie Bauer, Seattle. Now *there* was a leisure consumer product we might look into.

You cannot buy a company just by looking at its financial reports. You must make an on-site review. I selected a few men to accompany me and we flew to Seattle. As soon as I walked in the door, I could feel electricity. The people were happy in their work. They enjoyed making outdoorsman clothing and gear. The sons of the founder ran the business. They had not thought of selling the business, but when we brought up the subject and they saw that they could enjoy the outdoor life as much as they wanted to on the sales proceeds, they named a price. We negotiated and walked away owning Eddie Bauer. It proved to be one of General Mills's best acquisitions.

How did we come to buy Monet Jewelry? My wife bought some earrings which I admired. I asked her the name of the maker. On close examination, she found the name Monet. I looked them up and

People Power

found they were in New England. I took an attorney and an accountant and went out there. We inspected the facilities, but more importantly we met the people. They were creative, talented, and hard-working. We snooped around to find any clues as to whether the owners might be willing to sell. It turned out they were anxious to get out. Offers, counter-offers, negotiation — we bought Monet.

A secretary of mine came in one morning wearing a smart-looking outfit.

"Where did you buy it?" I asked after complimenting her. "Dayton's?"

"I got it through a catalogue," she replied.

I was amazed. Catalogue buying was a risk and usually did not turn out as well as the buyer expected.

"What catalogue?" I asked.

"I can't think of the name," she said, "but I'll bring it in tomorrow."

The next morning she had the catalogue opened to the picture of the outfit she had worn. The company was called Talbots. Another on-site inspection. Another discovery of competent, productive people. Another General Mills acquisition. We were now in the catalogue business.

We tried to buy another catalogue firm, Orvis, but they did not want to sell. We were frustrated because they were every bit as good as Talbots. We walked away empty-handed, but that is better than trying to force a reluctant owner to sell by offering a high price. You will never get what you think you are paying for when the people involved are not enthusiastic in their work. In any company, the people are just as important as the product!

People need to be taken care of no matter what. But that "no matter what" often proves to be a Catch-22. For instance, in the period prior to the liquidation of first our animal feed division and then nearly half of our flour mills, we were facing big trouble, In the year ending May 1962 our sales had dropped 5 percent and our profits had dropped a sickening 20 percent. Strong medicine was needed.

Said *Time* magazine, in its January 11, 1963 edition, ". . . Rawlings, 58, put General Mills through a harsh purge. In what some call 'Rawlings' earthquake,' he named six new division managers and four vice presidents. And he liquidated General Mills biggest liability —

its animal feed division..."

That "earthquake" rocked some 1,300 people from their jobs. But we had to do it in order to save the jobs of the other 13,000 employees. *Time* reported that in the first six months of our next fiscal year, although sales continued to decline some 6 percent, "profits rose an impressive 49 percent."

People at General Mills had felt threatened by me when I first arrived. Sgt. Summers, one of the van operators who helped me move, retired from the Air Force, and we hired him. He was a godsend to both me and Mrs. Rawlings as expediter and handyman. Next, my former aide, James Summer, became available, and I hired him. That worked out particularly well as he later became President of General Mills. Frank Tenny was a former officer with AMC. We felt he could fill a requirement we had. He was an outdoorsman as I was, but that was not the requirement. I went after several more from the Air Force, and people at General Mills began to think I would be "militarizing" the company.

This misconception soon dissolved when it became apparent that I was bringing in talent I knew would make everybody's jobs more secure.

I was also concerned about the welfare of another group of people — our consumers. It was surprising to me to find that nowhere in General Mills's vast food products operations was there a formal, accredited nutritionist. The public was becoming more and more aware of the importance of nutrition. Health food restaurants and health food stores were springing up from coast to coast, and the food editors of newspapers were beginning to evaluate food products not just for taste and convenience, but also for nutritional value. I was in favor of this movement toward better nutrition and I decided to do something about it.

I remembered Dr. Douglas Talbott, whom I knew in Dayton, Ohio. I called him and he agreed to come to Minneapolis. He looked over our situation, saw the need, and agreed to search for a first-class nutritionist. A few weeks later he returned with a brochure on Dr. Ivy Celender. I looked over her training, experience, and photograph.

"What are we waiting for, Doug?" I asked. "She is just the professional we are searching for."

"There's a problem, Ed."

People Power

"It's certainly not her looks. They will do credit to Betty Crocker."

"No, it's her husband."

"What about him?"

"He's an artist at the National Gallery of Art in Washington. If he relocates, it will not be easy for him to find another spot." Dual-career families were not as commonplace then as they are now.

I thought a moment. We had fine Twin Cities art institutions and colleges. We at General Mills supported them with annual contributions. Maybe...

"Doug," I said, "can you have them both visit us? I may be able to solve the problem."

It took some doing, but Ivy came aboard General Mills and her husband joined the Minneapolis Institute of Arts until a faculty position at Macalester College was finalized. She proved to be a professional in every sense of the word, not only upgrading the nutritional value of our consumer food products but also enhancing dietary products of the Specialty Products Divison. To help you get a handle on the high level of her technical expertise, here she is talking about a product to medical editors:

"Dietetic Paygel P is supplied only at a professional level to doctors, clinics, and hospitals since it would have no place in the diet of a healthy person. But for those suffering from kidney disease... it means they can enjoy many of the foods they formerly could not eat... The wheat starch is first and foremost humanitarian but the relatively low cost measured against comparable products amounts to a very real saving for the institutions or families."

So we filled another need in our service to people, thanks to a person with education and ability.

My days as Chairman of the Board were numbered. I loved every single one of those days. Not because of the paperwork, but more because of the people work. Even though I was 63, I was still driven to seek out and be receptive to new ideas and then to encourage their use through change. In less than two years I would be 65, and forced to retire as Chairman of the Board. I brushed that thought aside.

I still had work to do.

Chapter XII

Enjoying the Fruits

If I sound like I came to General Mills, I saw, and I contributed, change that to *we* came, *we* saw. Pete was my constant source of inspiration and reinforcement. Without her, I could never have achieved what I did.

Art was alive and well in Minneapolis, but not as we had thought. At least there were no women's art clubs like the one to which she belonged in Dayton. And the antique collecting activity was practically non-existent. Apparently, the people who moved west to Ohio brought their belongings with them, but the people who moved to Minnesota were more self-reliant and industrious. No belongings today, no antiques tomorrow. Also, the native woods that grew in Ohio were more appreciated by antique enthusiasts: black walnut, cherry, and birch. So there were few antique shops or auctions in or around Minneapolis for myself or Pete to explore.

There were no officers' wives clubs or other women's organizations that interested her. You might say it was quite an environmental shock for her to move from Dayton to Minneapolis. In Dayton she was the "mother superior." All the ladies would look to her for advice, and she was always surrounded by friends. When she came to Minneapolis, she knew nobody. She felt out in the cold. I was busy as all get out, and she was on her own. It was a rough transition for her. It would be for any wife placed in that same position.

Enjoying the Fruits

What filled the vacuum largely for her was her painting. She really blossomed as a painter, both in quality and in quantity. She did not promote her art. She painted for the love of it. Still, without participating in gallery exhibits, she occasionally sold her work. Somebody who visited us would take a liking to her work and buy a painting. Many were painted for our four sons and their families and were waiting for them when they visited.

Family and home were the major beneficiaries of her free time, and I made sure I received my share. I always tried to remember to give my wife credit when interviewed by the media. There's an old maxim: "Without an understanding, resourceful wife behind him, no man can really be successful." I reiterate that now.

Even I began to have more free time. For one thing, I joined the Board of Directors of Weyerhaeuser Company, a company headquartered in Tacoma, Washington. My first contact with that company had been during World War II, when I met George Crosby. He was a large holder of Weyerhaeuser stock in those days and later served on the Board of Directors. The more I got to know the company as a Minneapolis neighbor, the more I appreciated the way it operated. Its reforestation and water pollution control plans, its respect for our natural resources, its concern for the public interest — all this impressed me.

Weyerhaeuser has remained, to this writing, of great personal interest to me. When asked by the reporter for Weyerhaeuser Magazine my reasons for accepting a position on their Board, I said, "Weyerhaeuser Company has lots of potential." I added with a chuckle, "I like to be on a winning team," but then in a more serious vein I explained my fervent desire to contribute to that company's success. I hope I have.

It was broadening to see the differences in the two companies. A building project at General Mills might run two to ten million dollars. At Weyerhaeuser, it was not unusual to have one for five hundred million dollars.

At General Mills, seeds were planted and harvested for food in a matter of months. At Weyerhaeuser, a fresh-planted seedling would not be harvested for twenty-five years.

However, they did have one thing on common — people. In Weyerhaeuser, just as in General Mills, I found that the key to effective operations was the individual. Through that commonality was I able to start immediately to make my contribution.

****

As to recreation, I visited Wondra Island and enjoyed hunting and fishing. I'll always remember one outing there which I arranged.

August is a good month to find people with leisure time. With the help of my staff I arranged a four-day Labor Day weekend for a mix of General Mills executives, other business executives, and retired Air Force generals. It was to be a weekend of camaraderie, cards, fishing, and the exchange of ideas.

Although the weekend was to be relatively free of organized acitivity, I invited Dr. Donaldson, head of the Department of Fisheries at the University of Washington. We had grown up together in Tracy, Minnesota, so I knew him well. I asked him to bring along the motion pictures he had taken of his many inspections of Bikini Atoll to appraise the effects of the atomic bomb on fish life. His team had done this over a number of years and had found that, if anything, fish life improved.

Knowing that General Power, former Commander of SAC, and General LeMay, former Chief of Staff, USAF, were deeply involved in atomic weaponry, I informed them of these films. They agreed to come, as did retired Generals Terry Morrison, Ira Eaker and Tooey Spaatz, the latter head of USAF in Europe during World War II and later Chief of Staff, USAF.

On the business side were executives including Harold Sweatt, Chairman and CEO of Honeywell; Fred Weyerhaeuser, Director of Weyerhaeuser; DeWayne Andreas, CEO of ADM; John Morehead, CEO at Northwestern National Bank; Thayer Tutt, CEO of Broadmoor Hotel; Don Knutson, CEO of Knutson Co.; Art Storz, CEO of Storz Brewery; and Earl Thacker, prominent business man from Hawaii. From the financial world came Herb Walker of New York and Alton Rainy of Little Rock, Arkansas. From General Mills came my fellow directors, Charlie Bell and Bill Lang, plus Sewell Andrews and Paul Parker.

Leisure time was something to be enjoyed, but also profited from. There is not doubt that everybody enjoyed those days on Won-

Enjoying the Fruits

dra Island, nor is there doubt that each benefited from the other's presence.

Of particular value was the military — business mix. Since I epitomized that duality, with one foot in the military and the other in the civilian business world, I was usually in the center of those give-and-takes.

We had just turned some trout into the kitchen, and had cleaned up and changed, when General LeMay sat down across from me and sounded me out. "If you had your choice, Ed, would you start your life in business or the military?"

"Whichever needed me most," I answered, neatly getting off the hook.

He persevered with, "Don't you miss flying?"

"I sure do. If I started my career as a civilian I might very well have become an airline pilot."

"Still, you did more business in the Air Force than you did flying."

"I clocked over 10,000 pilot hours. But you're right. I was in charge of what was probably the largest business in the world." I filled my pipe halfway, lit it, and puffed a few times on it. He pulled his chair closer.

"Ed, when you wanted something done in the Air Force, you gave an order and it was done. You can't give orders now. You have to convince department heads, get Board votes, lick boots. Doesn't that come hard to you?"

"Hey buddy," I replied, "people are people, in uniform or not."

"Are you saying you licked boots in the service?"

"Not really. What I'm saying is that I had just as much concern for people and winning their support and enthusiasm in Dayton as I now have in Minneapolis. I had the Chief of Staff to convince and I had to win Congressional votes. Same ball game."

"But Ed, when you first came to Dayton, you were faced with more civilians at Wright-Patterson than military. They were an obstacle. Did you go around and give them a pep talk? No, you terminated them." He waited while I puffed. He thought he had me treed.

"That was wartime, Curt," I replied. "I knew how to win those civilians over but it could take time. We did not have the time. So I did what had to be done."

LeMay pointed to Storz. "He says there's a war going on in the beer business all the time. And I heard Bell and Weyerhaeuser talking this morning — business is one competitive conflict after another. You're in a business war now, Ed, only you don't want to face up to it. Maybe you're getting soft in your old age!"

I laughed. Soft indeed! "How about a duel at sunrise, Curt. I challenge you to ten times around the island on foot."

He thought a moment. "Those trout gave us some fight this afternoon, didn't they, Ed?"

"Seriously, Curt," I continued, "it *is* easier to work with personnel in the military; you're right but with the wrong reason. You and I picked the right people for the job. If they got transferred to a higher priority and the substitute turned out to be the wrong man, we could move out that person fairly easily without hurting him. Within a civilian organization, it is more difficult to make these transfers. There is greater specialization. An engineer can't be put in merchandising. I have three choices: I could fire him. That's a hurtful thing. I can move him to another equivalent job, if such exists. Or I can promote him out of the way. I favor two and three. Not because I'm soft, but because I'm human. I was human in the military, too, Curt."

He slapped his knee. "I wish you were still there, Ed."

If my son, Gerry, had not come along with some proposals for the evening, I'd bet Curtis LeMay and I would still be debating it.

****

To better serve the consumer seeking leisure time products, we formed a new division at General Mills — the Craft, Game, and Toy Division. Its aim was to give families the opportunity to make better use of their leisure time, not waste it. I have already mentioned Parker Brothers, Inc. as one of the first acquisitions in that field because it was a foundation post of that division.

My comments to the press on the new division at that time were:

"The company's commitment to growth has led General Mills to explore opportunities in fields other than its traditional food business. We think that there is great compatibility between our high quality and consumer-oriented food business as represented by Betty Crocker

Enjoying the Fruits

and Big G cereals and the marketing of wholesome, quality consumer products in the fast-growing leisure time activities industry. This new division gives us the necessary organization to harness our combined resources more effectively so that we can grow in the right way."

The entry of General Mills into the leisure time field had been an outgrowth of the concept developed by our group called the Venture Team, headed by Louis Polk, our data processing chief. It fostered an operating philosophy that the company could successfully develop new business areas in high growth fields, a prime one of which was leisure activity.

I have already mentioned Rainbow Crafts and its Play-Doh modeling compound. They also produced Playnts Poster Paints, We did pretty well in these. We did well, too, with Craft Master, enabling us to get involved in the fast-growing hobby and crafts area by offering paint-by-number sets and model hobby kits. The manager of the new division was Craig A. Nalen, a graduate of both Princeton University and Stanford University's School of Business Administration. He reported directly to Polk.

One of Polk's jobs was to evaluate all acquisitions on an intensive basis. If we found that we had bought the wrong company, there was no fixing of blame and therefore no need for the people who made the buying decision to have to defend that decision. We were free to act strategically and with dispatch. We sold the mistake at the earliest possible moment. In that way, we kept the results of our acquisitions at a high rate of profitability.

Of course, the focus of our attention remained on the mianstream of our business, consumer foods. Building those profits was our priority. Even our office complex in Golden Valley just outside of Minneapolis helped brand name recognition. We built a lot of Betty Crocker interest and prestige with the seven Betty Crocker kitchens in that building. People came from all over the country to visit those kitchens. The kitchens were named Pennsylvania Dutch, Cape Cod, California, Chinatown, Williamsburg, Arizona Desert, and Hawaiian.

Visitors were given a tour of the facilities and were able to view our research facilities, our quality control, and our production techniques. They came away with free samples and free recipes. We occasionally asked them to taste-test a new recipe. What some companies had to use (wide-flung market surveys in order to determine consumer preference at a great cost in time and money), we could do practically overnight at hardly any cost.

This marrying of research and recipe development worked out very well. Eventually some 70,000 people visited these seven kitchens each year. Unfortunately, this size was its undoing. It became too unwieldy and expensive to accommodate such large numbers. It was interfering with the efficiency of the kitchens. This was long after I left. In November, 1984, the kitchens were closed to the public.

We guarded and protected every one of our trademarks and brand names. Any start-up of brand name that came close enough to confuse the consumer would ring an alarm in our legal office. Attorney letters would go out. If that did not deter the culprits, court action soon did.

One important brand is Wheaties. Ronald Reagan worked as an announcer for a Des Moines, Iowa, radio station back in the twenties when our Wheaties commercials were on that station. I still tell my friends that Ronald Reagan once pushed Wheaties.

Other Big G cereals were Cheerios and Total. Cereals were a huge market. But consumers demand variety, so we never sat on our laurels. Continual innovation and aggressive marketing were the order of the day. My own sense of drive was reflected as a sense of urgency in the company.

It was a matter of urgency that we provided consumers with products superior to the competition. It was a matter of urgency that we demonstrated that superiority in growing consumer preference and therefore a growing share of the market.

Yes, we played the game with numbers. But we never forgot who the players really were. We made sure that our people enjoyed their work and were also motivated with their own feeling of drive and pride in winning. The enthusiasm we generated at Board meetings was not permitted to die there. We looked for ways to pass that excitement to middle management and thence to the individual worker, be it in sales, in production, or in auxiliary services.

We ran contests, gave certificates of recognition, planned parties and banquets, encouraged employee clubs and hobbies — all in addition, of course, to the usual pay raises, bonuses, and promotions.

The result was less a management-labor relationship of confrontation and more a management-labor relationship of cooperation.

Enjoying the Fruits

I'm talking about the late sixties and early seventies. Today such a movement is the "in" thing. At that time, however, it was revolutionary, and there were old-timers with whom we had to compromise in order to make progress. So progress was slow.

Our employees still had a sense of fun and excitement. One event was an annual TOUCHDOWN sales contest. Each division and operation was given the freedom to set its own rules and regulations for participation in the contest. We felt that was more fun than trying to adapt to and abide by complicated rules set by higher-ups. There was no overall company award. Each division determined the number of awards to be given within its own organization.

At a company dinner in Minneapolis, for which each winner received an all-expense-paid trip for himself or herself and spouse, I awarded each a President's Cup. It proved to be an exciting event.

Take 1967. I did not just launch it with a communique to all division heads and then sit back and wait for results. I followed up with phone calls and visits. The phone calls were not just to department heads, but also to people in the field. Travel had to fit in with time availability, but I remember visiting Los Angeles, San Francisco, and Chicago in that one year.

In Los Angeles, the "players" in TOUCHDOWN '67 called themselves the "Southern California Budget Busters." A huge sign on the wall said "Welcome Coach." Maybe they knew I was going to give them a halftime pep talk. Present were management representatives in that area for Flour and Food Service, Specialty Products, Chemicals, Grocery Products, and others. Wide participation was important.

Next stop was a noon meeting near San Francisco. There were some inside jokes, lots of back-slapping, some inspirational words on my part, and a strong feeling of team camaraderie among Food and Flour, Grocery, Chemicals, and me.

The following day I flew to Chicago for a dinner meeting. Grocery Products, Flour and Food Service, Chemicals and Specialty Products were all represented. There were reminders from division leaders that TOUCHDOWN '67 would end within a month. I expressed my wish that all could be winners and attend the gala President's Cup Dinner at the Radisson Hotel in Minneapolis on December 11. I reminded them that the winners would have their expenses paid and would hear as principal speaker not me, but the Reverend Bob Richards, director of the Wheaties Sports Federation.

Little wonder that we had few labor strikes, and those few that we had were short-lived.

Not only was the company becoming larger and showing greater profits, but I was also benefiting financially. During my tenure, there were several stock splits, two and sometimes three-for-one.

I became more interested in local charities, not just from the company's viewpoint, but from my personal desire to support them. Boy Scouts and Girl Scouts were perennials, and there were also those that were less well-known though no less important.

One of these was Chileda Habilitation Institute in LaCrosse, Wisconsin. They helped physically handicapped children. I mean really helped. I saw some who were so helpless they could not go to the bathroom without assistance, but after a period of physical therapy they were almost self-sufficient in all such basic activities. The Institute held an annual run. It required the serving of some two thousand breakfasts. General Mills donated pancake mix and syrup. Later, when we entered the growing yogurt field, that product was also donated to the breakfast. If there was any hesitation on the part of new people at General Mills later, I made the necessary contribution myself.

The retired Air Force officers were doing the same thing from their headquarters in Bozeman, Montana. I am still delighted to help with the Institutes activities. It is certainly distressing to know that one in one thousand births is a physically handicapped child! At this writing, General Mathis heads up this worthy project.

The more you do, the more you can do. Looking back now, I wonder how I had time to take part in charitable activities; company management; civic activities like the Minneapolis Safety Council; and still have time to serve on many Boards of Directors, including Northwest Bancorporation and the North Star Research and Development Institute, both in Minneapolis; the American Ordnance Association in Washington, D.C.; the Cox Coronary Heart Institute in Dayton; the National Industrial Conference Board in New York City; and the American Management Association. There were also educational in-

Enjoying the Fruits

stitution boards where I occasionally attended meetings. And I served on the Businessmen's Committee of the U.S. Olympic Committee.

What did I do in my spare time? I enjoyed time with my wife and at the Minneapolis Club, the Hazeltine National Golf Club, and the Wayzata Country Club. I hunted and I fished. I enjoyed visits by my four sons and their families: Captains Peter, Charles (Gerry), Richard, and Second Lieutenant John. Occasionally there was a reunion and occasionally a christening. Let's see, I believe I was up to eight grandchildren before those less-than-two years as Chairman of the Board were over.

In September, 1968, I recommended to the Board of Directors that President James P. McFarland succeed me as Chief Executive Officer and that James A. Summer, then serving as Executive Vice President, be elected to the Board, effective immediately. This came as a surprise to many of the directors.

"In contemplation of my retirement next year," I explained, "I feel the need to begin the orderly transfer of corporate responsibility to younger members of our management team. I know that these men are ready and able to lead General Mills to continued growth and service."

The Board voted yes.

Two months later I announced my retirement as Chairman of the Board, to take effect January 1st, 1969: "During this past year General Mills has made the management moves necessary to provide it with aggressive and forward-looking executive leadership in the years ahead. This is an appropriate time for me to step aside, and I do so with complete confidence that the Company will continue its growth and service. My plans are to remain in Minneapolis where I hope I can devote considerably more time to community affairs.

And that's exactly what I did.

The newspapers reported that statement of mine and a financial statement of the Company. The *Minneapolis Tribune* noted that the net earnings rose from $16.7 million in 1964 to $31.3 million in 1968 and per share earnings went from 80 cents to $1.79. There were many other media stories reaching out even to my own home town. The *Tracy Headlight-Herald* headlined its story, "This Grad Helped Build Successful General Mills."

What surprised me the most were the favorable comments in

the magazine, *Southwestern Miller*. After all, the divestiture was not a particularly beneficial move for them. Their comments in the January 14, 1969, issue were:

"In his direction of General Mills, General Rawlings in the finest sense embodied the professional management ideal that flour millers have come in recent years to seek with increasing vigor. ...General Rawlings did not gain a widespread acquaintance among American millers. This did not preclude deep admiration in the industry of his business acumen which brought a soaring of General Mill's earnings to successive record highs. ...Certainly, wherever millers meet in the future, the conversation almost inevitably will turn to the 'Rawlings era.' Few men have retired leaving such an imprint on milling; none has meant more to industry's thinking about its future course."

A retirement dinner was held at the Lafayette Club on Monday, January 27, 1969. When I was not enjoying the corn soup, prime sirloin steak, wild rice, and fresh asparagus, I was enjoying the remarks of Charlie Bell, Jim McFarland, and Paul Parker. Gerald "Spike" Kennedy broke us up with his talk, a parody on everybody there.

A number of letters of good wishes were read. Not read but handed to me were some letters from folks in Tracy, military men from Dayton days, and other old friends — letters that I keep, reread, and treasure to this day. Telegrams were read from Senator Walter F. Mondale, Congressman Clark MacGregor, and others.

It may have been a milestone for General Mills. But I did not consider it as a milestone in my life.

I still looked forward to years of service on the General Mills Board of Directors. I had all of those other boards to which I could now give more of my time. Air Force organizations needed support. Education was a growing interest through my service on university boards.

It was not really an end. It was a beginning.

PART IV

Chapter XIII

Computer Consortium

One letter I received was from Townsend McAlpin in New York. He wrote, "I read the other day that you were retiring as Chairman of the Board of General Mills and somehow found it hard to visualize you as really being 'in retirement.' Maybe you really mean it, but I can't help but feel I will read where you have popped up as the head and spark plug of some go-go company."

He was right. Except it was not a company. It was a consortium.

Remember this. I was born to fly. I flew in Dayton. I flew in Hawaii. Even when I was at the Pentagon with standby crews ready to fly me anywhere, I finagled my way into the pilot's seat every chance I got.

When I became a civilian and worked for General Mills, I let their pilots do the piloting. I resolved that safety dictated this. They knew their planes just as I had known Air Force planes. So I took a back seat. My desire to fly began to cry for a mode of expression. Perhaps that was the real energy behind my drive.

Certainly I sought to be successful in every project I undertook. Certainly I applied all of my knowledge and experience to get every project I undertook off the ground. But that extra boost which brought higher and higher profits and faster and faster goal attainment could very well have been at least partially powered by my desire to rise above the usual man's-eye-view horizons.

If I could no longer do it in an aircraft, I found expression in business craft.

Leaving the chairmanship at General Mills did not mean my leaving behind that drive to be "airborne." I just had to find a new vehicle. Frankly, I had found it even before I left; I would help higher education fly to new heights.

McAlpin was right. I could not retire. I do not believe in retirement. I have seen too many men retire and go into decline. The mental attitude of ending your creative work seems to be an invitation for life to end. I was still busy. I had things to do.

I was serving on a number of company boards, university boards, and national boards. There were Air Force projects I was interested in, charitable organizations I now could devote more time to, and recreation in which I could indulge more frequently — like hunting.

Looking back on my retirement dinner at General Mills, it was almost like the Last Supper must have been. No happiness, no glee. Just somber sadness. Previously, when I had participated in the retirement dinners of other executives, it was the same story over and over. The retiree is dropped like a hot rock and soon forgotten.

This is a great loss of talent. I resolved it would not be my lot. Rather than ask the question standard to retirees, "What do I do with myself now?" I asked, "How do I best use my talents now?"

One thing was sure. I would remain as close as I could to where the action was. So I proceeded to work out consulting arrangements, first with Magnetic Controls on whose Board I had served for ten years; next with General Mills on whose Board I continued to serve for seven years after my retirement as its Chairman; then with Knutson Companies, a contracting firm whose owner, Don Knutson, I knew well; and also with Weyerhaeuser on whose Board I had already served some twelve years. I continued to serve on the Board of the Foley Manufacturing Company.

That first year "in retirement" I built a consulting practice that would have been the envy of a man fifty years my junior. I was busy morning to night helping solve the same kinds of problems that I had experienced all my life.

In addition, I remained on the Board of the Air Force Academy Foundation; the Board of the Civilian/Military Institute; and on

Computer Consortium

the Board of the Falcon Foundation which is dedicated to helping young men and women prepare for the Air Force Academy through scholarships, counselling and moral support. Incidentally, this is the only board I know of whose members pay one hundred dollars a year to serve. I informed the Air Force Chief of Staff that I was holding myself ready for special tasks that could be useful to the Air Force.

So it was that I kept one foot in the military world and one foot in the business world — the two areas in which I was both interested and knowledgeable.

I was still able to make more time for family — my grandchildren count was now up to eight — and I was still able to go hunting.

It was natural that my many years of involvement with General Mills would make that company my main focus even in retirement. How could I sit at the same table with the same directors, only a few feet from where I sat as Chairman, and not remain involved in helping to solve problems; evaluate proposed acquisitions or divestitures; and attempt to enhance public relations, employee relations, and community relations.

The Board appoints committees of its own members to handle specific areas of concern and to report back to the Board as a whole for action. I served on two: the Board's Executive and Responsibility Committees. I also served on a separate General Mills Board whose responsibility it was to administer employee benefits. General Mills provided me with an office and secretary to assist with these responsibilities.

If that paints a picture of a man in retirement, then perhaps I was redefining the word. Hopefully my new definition will become more and more the accepted one in business, industry, professional and military: an experienced person who continues to share the wisdom of that experience wherever invited regardless of age.

My successor at General Mills, James P. McFarland, extended an open invitation to me by providing me with that office, a standard benefit since the company was formed in 1928. Later, when I retired from the Board in 1976, he showed no remorse when he said, "Few men have been able in one lifetime to serve so brilliantly and successfully in two different careers... in the 17 years which General Rawlings spent with our company he provided imagination and leadership which have made our continued growth and progress possible. The General Mills of today and the General Mills of tomorrow will continue to bear the stamp of his ideas and philosophy."

The office they provided me became a sounding board for the General Mills of tomorrow. Many an enjoyable pipe was puffed by me as Jim McFarland or Charlie Bell or some other executive chatted with me about a matter of import. Sometimes I could contribute nothing. Other times, my experience provided just the insight needed at the moment.

The acquisition program that I had spearheaded in 1967, leading the company into snack foods; crafts, games, and toys; the fashion industry and direct marketing; was continued by Jim. There were some hair-thin choices to make. Some involved more the evaluation of people than of numbers, bringing experience higher in priority.

When you put new tires on your car, you might say the car has been re-tired. I was more that kind of re-tired. I was ready for a lot more mileage.

* * * *

Even after I retired from the Board, I continued to do what I could, working out of that office. But the emphasis changed. My General Mills contacts tapered off and my contacts with education increased. As a student of computers myself all through the years, I had watched their growing applications in our society. I began to wonder what would happen to Americans as we all became dependent on computers, whether we knew it or not, or wanted it or not.

But education was not responding. A dismal gap in University curricula was computer terminology and use.

Computers were my "aide de camp" in Washington, Dayton, and Minneapolis. When I served on the Boards of Hamline University in St. Paul, and Mills College in Oakland, California, computers were conspicuous by their absence. Ditto, would you believe, at the Air Force Academy!

How high could higher education really get without computers in the computer age? It took me a number of years to realize the wide extent of this problem. I explored all levels of education and was not able to find a single school in the seventies dealing with computer literacy, except technical schools that were training program-

Computer Consortium

mers, electronic trouble-shooters, and technicians.

The standard question and reply went like this.

"How can you afford not to teach the language and use of computers, Mr. Dean?"

"We cannot afford to acquire them, General."

This was a national problem. A generation of young people was being launched into business, professional, and military life with a gaping hole in its "wing." I resolved to start with the university I knew best, Hamline. This was now in the late seventies.

I went to see the President of Hamline University, Dr. Jerry Hudson. After appropriate small talk, I hit him with the standard question. He retaliated with the standard answer. This time I was ready.

I took out my personal checkbook and wrote a check for $10,000. I handed it to him.

"How much is that check for?" I asked.

"Ten thousand," he replied, adding, "A very generous gift, General."

"Look again," I said. "It's really for $20,000." After his eyebrows raised, forming a quizzical look, I explained, "General Mills Foundation will match this donation."

He smiled broadly. "We can really make a start with $20,000."

"What kind of a start?" I wanted to make sure he would take off properly and get the project off the ground.

"This will pay for some basic equipment and for the summer salaries of a few key members of the staff. They can put together a course curriculum by September for faculty approval. We can be teaching a computer course by our next semester."

"Credit?"

"Yes, it will be a credit course. But not a required course, at least not for starters."

"What about equipment?" I asked. I was back to the standard question and got the standard answer all over again — money only for the simplest system.

"But with a computer course going, Jerry, you'll have more students, more money, more reason to budget sophisticated computer equipment to teach the course," I insisted.

"You're absolutely right. But, as you know, it will take not only the education of our students but the education of our Board members."

Rawlings

Yes, I knew. "Count on me as a one-man team to begin that job," I assured him. We shook hands and I left, already planning my strategy.

The faculty had left for summer vacation, but Jerry Hudson was able to convince those key members to return. In the next two months they put together a solid course outline for "Computer Literacy." It was approved by the faculty and immediately attracted good-sized classes. No other school, to my knowledge, was doing anything in the computer field.

Some years later, Hamline made their Computer Literacy course required in order to get a degree. This was in 1982, for the graduating class of 1986.

Between the mid-1970s and mid-1980s, there were big changes in my life including the death of my wife, my move to Hawaii, my battle against a life-threatening illness, and my re-marriage. But I am still so gung-ho on this computer project; let me continue with that story before I return to those events.

Once I saw Hamline under way with a computer literacy course, I began to visit other private colleges and universities, starting with those closest to me in Minnesota. Now I was able to cite Hamline's steps as an inducement for others to dare to put their academic necks on the line. The risk was less.

Standard question. Standard answer.

Two people at Control Data became my allies in the crusade: William Keye, a Hamline trustee with me and who was also on the Control Data Board; and William Norris, a man whom I had known at Sperry Univac long before he left there to found Control Data. They armed me with the ammunition I needed to make a dent in status quo thinking.

Education can be likened to a sleeping, monolithic giant. It takes a lot of push and shove to get it to move. The resistance to change is greater than in the military or in industry. Educators in higher education talk a lot about innovation, but few are daring enough to rock the boat.

I acquired more allies. They came by the hundreds of thousands from an unexpected direction. The year that Hamline started the first university computer course, there were an estimated 30,000 elementary and secondary schools in the United States using com-

Computer Consortium

puters for instruction.

An army of high school graduates with their computer appetites whetted were heading for colleges and universities in the fall of 1982 with expectations of continuing to expand their knowledge of and use of computers, only to find that higher education was lower in that field of education.

I visited the College of St. Thomas in St. Paul. The Dean there admitted, "One student asked me yesterday where the student word processing computer was located. She said she had learned to use one at high school. I had to admit that we did not have one of those yet."

I did not invite the standard answer with the standard question. Nor did I whip out my checkbook and write another $10,000 check. Instead of planting more seed money, I decided to try to reap a bigger crop from the seed money I already sowed.

There was a new president at Hamline, Dr. Charles J. Graham. I visited him and discussed the problem of high schools being the dead end of computer education.

"Hamline is showing the way," I reminded him, "but nobody is looking."

"We can't interfere with the policy of other institutions," he maintained.

"Yes, you can," I insisted. "But instead of interfering, how about running interference?"

"This isn't a football game, General."

"No, but it's an education game. Hamline has a computer course. You have successfully evaded the tacklers whose apathy could have obstructed that course. Other colleges are faced with the same apathy, the same shortage of funds, the same disinclination to change that Hamline rose above. As educators, don't you think it is your obligation to share that know-how with at least the other private colleges and universities in this State of Minnesota?"

"I can't say no to that, General, but how do I go about it within the context of protocol?"

"Write the Minnesota colleges; tell them what you have done; ask them to share what they are planning to do."

He thought a moment. "You mean form a sort of educational consortium?"

The words exploded like a bomb in my mind. Its energy was joy and exultation, energy that I directed in gratitude to God.

"Of course," I replied.

He wrote the letter.

The idea of an educational consortium was not new in Minnesota. Some seven years previously, the Minnesota State Legislature began funding the Minnesota Educational Computer Consortium. Its purpose was to promote computers as instructional tools in state elementary and secondary school classrooms. The MECC created a time-sharing network so that these schools could share computing facilities. It was a nonstandard answer to the standard question, one that higher education institutions might themselves learn a lesson from.

As a result of Hamline's letter to Minnesota's private colleges, a number quickly joined the computer consortium of higher education. They were St. Thomas, St. Johns, St. Catherine's, Augsburg, and Macalester. The consortium was born.

There was no fee to the participating college or university. Their only obligation was to share their progress in adopting computers into their educational program including any breakthrough, innovation, or improved way of using computers in higher education.

Hamline offered to be the consortium's monitor, at least at the start, and to compile the information in a bulletin for easy review by the members.

The newsletter got started. The six initial members began their contributions to it, each contribution helping the others to expand their own computer uses in the classroom.

I used this success now to go out for bigger game. I went national. One uses one's "connections." It is not exploitation; it is following the path of least resistance. I offered membership in the consortium to Mills College and they joined. So did my other alma mater, Harvard Business School. Then, through my connection with the United States Air Force Academy, it joined. And, with members like that, how could Dartmouth refuse, and Stanford, and...

In September 1985 the consortium newsletter, appropriately titled "The Rawlings Computer Connection," contained some exciting news about computer progress in higher education. Here are some examples:

Harvard Business School reported that it began an intensive

Computer Consortium

program in 1983, in the use of personal computers. Initially they were used in an executive educational program, a program with a relatively small number of faculty involved. The success was so striking they moved quickly to the full MBA. Every MBA student was equipped with a personal computer. Only about ten percent of these students had any difficulty using them, but this corresponded to the percentage of students who had difficulty in numbers to start with.

Harvard Business School, realizing that early training in the use of personal computers was crucial, combined that training with analysis of a typical marketing case in the first two weeks of the semester. I remember how difficult I had found case-working at Harvard Business School until I got the hang of it. Computers then would have been a great help.

The single most important finding, according to the faculty member reporting to the newsletter, was "Using the PC's as an analytical tool to improve case analysis in ways that enable more thorough and penetrating discussion and lead to more valuable student insights." His report concluded with "the impact of bringing personal computers into the business education programs has proven bigger, more complex, and more rewarding than anticipated."

Could any university faculty read that and not wonder if they might be missing the boat?

How about the U.S. Air Force Academy. Well, you'd expect a faster start here where modern Air Force officers learn to develop, fly, and procure computer-based or computer-controlled aircraft, missiles, spacecraft, and battle management systems. So it was that, since 1981, the Air Force Academy has had a mainframe computer coupled with forty graphic terminals for use in a number of departments. For instance the Physics Department used them in simulations, tutorials, and drills. The Foreign Language Department used them in video-based tutorials.

In 1984, as a result of a faculty committee recommendation (presumably at least in part inspired by the information supplied by our consortium), the U.S. Air Force Academy began to install a network of modern microcomputers serving every dormitory room and office! This is not an overnight process, even for the Air Force. It is still going on at this moment but here is the gratifying year-to-year progress:

1984 - 290 microcomputers are installed in academic and staff areas giving the faculty and staff a chance to develop materials and prototype courses.

1985 - A basic computer science programming course begins using the microcomputers.

1986 - Microcomputer labs are established for cadet use. Other courses increase the use of microcomputers. A local area network is installed.

1987 - Completion of the installation of microcomputers in all cadet dormitory rooms, tied to the local area network.

I do not want to appear to take credit for this. But it is a good example of how one person's initiative can lead to monumental results, like a stone dropping into quiet waters and sending out ripples in ever expanding circles.

It was valuable to disseminate what the big boys were doing, but the smaller colleges and universities were busy, too, and their accomplishments were even more meaningful in terms of importance to that larger number of institutions, via the consortium newsletter.

Mills College, a small liberal arts college for women, had established a masters degree program in computer science skills back in 1981. With grants received from a number of foundations and companies. Mills upgraded its central academic computer to a VAX 11/780 system in January 1984. A technology research committee was then formed to evaluate proposed programs and discuss directions and goals. By fall of that year that committee identified and spelled out a college-wide microcomputer plan. A program of workshops was launched giving faculty hands-on experience with four different microcomputer systems. After one year of faculty familiarization and another year of faculty experimentation, Mills College then began to provide additional student and faculty access to database tools, electronic communication, and word processing.

My own Hamline University, also a small liberal arts university, was in the same basic position as Mills: it had a small student body with no major concern for the technical disciplines. Nevertheless, with the help of the seed money I described, Hamline did institute computing at a high quality level in their science programs, and this led to computer-intensive courses in disciplines that extended

Computer Consortium
across the curriculum.

Whether it was my proselytizing with the Board, or the Board's with the administration, or the administration's with the faculty, we will never know; but the faculty was convinced at an early date that computer science held a basic importance in liberal education.

As a result of this unique philosophy computer literacy was required for all students in the baccalaureate program beginning in 1982; then in the special courses; and soon there was a campus environment in which students were expected to use the computer in their work and faculty members were expected to do likewise in their course development.

What about that standard question and that standard answer? Well, Hamline committed more and more of its own resources in recent years, augmented by gifts and foundation grants. I am proud of my alma mater. Hamline continues to make an intensive effort to provide its student body with access and opportunities to use the computer in the development of their skills as informed leaders in a technical society.

My friend Bill Keye of the Hamline Board did yeoman service. Not long after I committed $10,000 to Hamline, matched by General Mills, Keye's Control Data pledged $50,000 in computer hardware, software, and staff services to the pilot project. Nor did he stop there. He had Control Data representatives calling on Minnesota colleges, as I was, urging them to consider joining the computer literacy consortium. He sincerely believed in the consortium.

"If we are to have an impact on computer literacy in higher education," he said, "the program must not be confined to one university nor to the traditional disciplines like math and science. Students in the humanities have to be involved, too." To which I said, "Go!"

* * * *

And then there were eight.

No, not eight colleges. Eight grandchildren. One's family, young and old, is a welcome respite from the business world.

All work and no play is dulling even to a "retired" person. How about a weekend at Wondra? Or a trip to Colorado to shoot ducks. Or eastern Washington?

Rawlings

During those busy retirement years in Minneapolis, I did all three, and more. Son Gerry and I took his camper and drove over the mountains to eastern Washington where there are a number of sloughs and creeks that the migrating ducks like.
We pitched camp and then put up a couple of blinds with a few decoys in front. Soon the mallards began to arrive and we shot our limit in short order. Another time we went to some backwaters near there owned by Weyerhaeuser. This was pass shooting. It was a lot of fun for both of us, but it did not net many ducks.

Thayer Tutt and I drove down to some hot springs in Colorado on the eastern side of the Rockies. The springs were full of watercress that the ducks loved. That was a lot of fun, too, and again we easily filled our limit.

And there were the trips to Arkansas, too. It was great fun to wait beside a water hole surrounded by hundred-foot pin oaks and then see the mallards flutter down. It was no trick to get one's limit. A boy named Pig Tail — his parents hoped this handsome 13th child would be the end — retrieved the ducks and then dressed them, or as he called it, 'pick 'em.' When I brought along my Chesapeake Bay Retriever, Chocolate, that dog beat Pig Tail to every duck. No cripple got away. Pig Tail really began to feel left out. Finally, when he could stand this competition no longer, he said, "General, I hope Chocolate doesn't learn to pick 'em, too."

Alton's cook was named Calvin. He could cook the best "hush puppies" you ever tasted. And then there was his guide Giggs. Giggs was a great caller. He could sound more like a duck than a duck could. He could also call racoons, fox, squirrels, owls, and hawks.

We enjoyed hunting out of Raney's camp for a number of years. Tons of stress must have been unloaded there. The only reason I stopped going was the federal limit on ducks was reduced to four. After that, it just was not worth the long trip.

Every year Pete and I would visit Hawaii at least once so she could be with her family. But these visits became fewer after her three brothers and her mother had passed away and all that were left were nieces and nephews. I always did like Hawaii. I, too, had nieces and nephews here and one sister-in law, all of whom I liked very much. So Hawaii called to me.

But so did Steamboat, Colorado. My son John built a duplex

Computer Consortium

there in those beautiful mountains. I put up the money and he contributed the labor. I frankly don't like to share a house with family. You lose your privacy and freedom. But, in this case, John rented his half of he duplex and lived in another house. So we had an ideal summer house; it always made me feel closer to nature.

John is a builder. He built the original house on speculation, intending to sell it, until I talked him out of it. He also built the house he lived in. Steamboat held promise for a builder then because of the expanding winter ski business, but now that has reached the saturation point and my son is relocating to Seattle where the building business is more diversified and active.

In Steamboat I enjoy working the waters of those small streams for trout and taking strolls through the woods. As it is some 7,000 feet high, the temperature is comfortable in the summer and people come from all over to escape the heat.

Getting back to computers, the way Bill Keye was driven to approach other Minnesota colleges, and the way I was driven to go out-of-state approach a number of colleges where I had suitable contacts, so too was I driven in 1987 to venture out of the country to approach a Canadian university and a Mexican university.

I had more than just an idea. Now I had a written record of how universities large and small were making use of computers in their teaching and how they were teaching the use of computers. I had real case studies: how St. Catherine's first credit course, Introduction to Computing, was filled in record time from its inception. How Augsburg College elevated its computer science minor to a major. How the St. Thomas computer science major is now second in attendance only to its business course.

I could share these strategies with universities all over the United States. I went to work to do exactly that. Today we have the University of Hawaii, the University of Alaska, Northern Washington, Eastern Washington, University of Puget Sound, Willamette, Ohio Wesleyan, Miami University of Ohio, George Washington University, Tufts, Dartmouth, and more in the consortium.

I could share these strategies with educators in Canada and south of the border. Thanks to the consortium the information was available. Now we have the University of Alberta and the University of Mexico.

"Yes," they said in Canada.
"Yes," they said in Mexico.
The consortium is now international.

Chapter XIV

Future Military Management

It is my purpose in this chapter to distill the essence of my experiences and actions in first the Air Corps and then the Air Force to reiterate their meaning that the best of them may be perpetuated.

Although many of the innovations have become largely standard operating procedures, the initial purposes need to be rekindled now in the minds of those using these procedures, lest the apathy that comes with anything "standard" renders them sterile.

In the chapter after this, I will attempt to do the same thing from my experiences and actions in business. Here again what may become accepted truisms can become so taken for granted that they become lost in complacency.

At the outset I must may pay tribute to the wisdom and foresight of those with whom I worked in the period 1946-1951, my comptrollership period: to such fine leaders as Mr. Lovett; Mr. Symington; the late General Arnold; General Spaatz; General Eaker; and General Vandenberg.

It is interesting to note that the Air Force comptrollership existed for three years before Congress adopted legislation that made it official. Therein lies the seed of my first recommendation.

Somebody has to run with the ball and risk getting tackled. A good idea, waiting to be born, may never see the light of day if somebody does not have the courage to help it along.

That may seem to be running afoul of existing practices or setting unprescribed precedent. Somebody once said that laws are made to be intelligently broken. I am not necessarily endorsing that, but a synonym for standard procedures is status quo. If we are to make progress, somebody has to stick his neck outside of the status quo. True, it may get chopped off. But if the men I mentioned earlier had not dared to implement the comptrollership, military management could still be in the Dark Ages.

They did not wait for Congressional approval of the details. Congress had already expressed the concept but not the details. They saw what needed to be done and they did it, as much within the context of existing protocol as they could remain.

Later, when as comptroller I was organizing workable budgetary procedures and needed electronic data processing assistance, I, too, did what needed to be done, as much within accepted practice as possible. I found a budget item called industrial research and transferred $100,000 to the Census Bureau faced with the same needs as ours. That led to the UNIVAC, and the first UNIVAC led to a lot of problems being solved in record time both for Census and Air Force.

Can you imagine the number of newspapers that could have been sold if reporters had decided to exploit it? I can just see the headlines: "General Misappropriates Funds," or "$100,000 Missing From Air Force Funds — Census Bureau Suspected."

There is no bravery like bravery on the battlefield, on the high seas, or in the skies. But our nation needs bravery behind the desk, too. Military men need to dare to be innovative, efficient, and creative even if some noses get bent out of shape in the process. To do otherwise — to play it personally safe — is to endanger our nation.

There was no safe haven in the Comptroller's office. We were treading untrod ground every step of the way. One of the steps that had to be taken in order for my office to avoid being merely an ivory tower was that the Comptroller's assistance had to reach to the field. Despite the lack of Air Force regulations that spelled out my right to organize Comptroller activities at field levels, I did so anyhow.

We tested a Comptroller office at Langley Field, Virginia (a Tactical Air Command base) and at Turner Air Force Base in Albany, Georgia (a wing level base). I kept a close record on these two tests. My neck was out. They proved successful. It was no surprise

Future Military Management

to me, as I was using proven business principles. I don't claim bravery beyond the call of duty. I kept my supervisors informed. I involved others in the experiment, like creating an Assistant for Field Management. I enlisted Field Commander cooperation. If any bravery medals are to be awarded, they should go to them.

The success of these tests led to publication of Air Force Regulations 20-34 and 170-16 which made the actions retroactively legal, and established Comptroller organizations at major commands, subcommands and wings.

Who do you assign to these field organizations? Pilots? Navigators? No, we needed business-trained specialists. So, just the way we trained pilots and navigators, we had to initiate a management education program.

Never sell education short. On-the-job training may be great, but what if the jobs have not been identified yet? Special Controllership courses had to be devised which would later crystallize jobs to fill identified needs. We established these courses first at our own Air Force institutions: Air Tactical School, Air Command and Staff School, USAF Special Staff School, Air War College, and Air Force Institute of Technology; we initiated training at Lowry and Maxwell Air Force Base. We also tapped the resources at existing universities such as Stanford, Columbia, Harvard, Pittsburgh, and Pennsylvania.

Next, we were ready for a cost control system. It would apply industrial management principles to Air Force operations. But, wait a minute, you say, how is money a measure of military efficiency? How can you equate dollars with firepower, morale, and strategy?

It really boils down to money being at least a symbol of energy, if not an actual form of energy. For instance, we broke work performance into twenty-five separate functions and, based on past experience, were able to assign a standard or expected cost to each. Then, by comparing the actual cost per work unit accomplished to the expected cost, commanders had a reliable guide in measuring efficiency, making decisions, and taking action.

Cost analysis set the price of those pots and pans I sold at Dayton's Department Store and the price of the books, beer, and buttons at the Texas post exchange. Cost analysis is now recognized as an integral part of planning and programming U.S. Air Force operations from the Air Staff to field commands.

Human nature favors the status quo. Change is resisted. So the introduction of a modern business concept in the Air Force took tact, diplomacy, and a continuing recognition of where each person was coming from. If innovators expect to take the ball and run with it roughshod over everybody, they are in for a rude awakening. You must enlist people every forward step you take.

If you don't enlist people, you'll be put on their hit list. It is easier for opponents to succeed in stopping you than for you to succeed in getting there without them. It is so simple to put down a new idea, so hard to win support for it. The education of peers, colleagues, and friends up and down the line is the answer.

You would think UNIVAC would get immediate unanimous support. People did not understand the details of the problems it could solve. Only after we had it a while and were able to demonstrate how rapidly we could react to Congressional queries about the budget and to budget changes was that innovation totally accepted, and, of course, later cheered.

In the summer of 1950, when the personnel of the Air Staff were completely occupied with the Korean War operations, the Munitions Boards asked for a statement of Air Force requirements to carry out the Joint Chiefs war plan. Those busy people could have been faced with the choice of ignoring the needs of the troops or the request of the Munitions Board. Thanks to UNIVAC and the Comptroller's budget analysis system, that either-or situation did not exist. The mechanical computation procedures saved time and labor and the job could be done. It was done. And it was done fast!

Congress is often a colleague needing to be educated. Iacocca of Chrysler Motors found that out when he appealed for a federal loan guarantee for the company. But that was rare. The military is in daily touch with Congress via their Pentagon offices. This kind of educating, of your Capitol Hill peers and colleagues, is often the most difficult. Hearing rooms are designed so that the committees sit on a raised platform. You are a witness but you feel more like the accused. Batteries of television lights focus on you. They are an intimidating factor.

Each Congressman on a committee has a different approach. Sometimes it is related to the interests of his own back-home constituency, sometimes to a particular national interest, but always to his

Future Military Management

own personality and style. As an educator on the stand before a Congressional action, you had better do your homework — know your subject and know your committee members.

I will never forget my first exposure to the House of Representatives. It was when the Air Corps was still a part of the Army. I was in the gallery with Army Budget Officer General Richards (now deceased). He had a friend on the Appropriations Committee who conducted the hearing. He kept sending his friend written notes. The Congressman from Michigan who chaired the Committee obviously saw that note passing and was riled by it. He got up and made a speech from the floor castigating General Richards and likening him to "an alley cat scratching dirt over his droppings." Of course, the note passing stopped.

I realized then that the hallowed halls of Congress were not only ringing with the strength of God but also with the frailties of men. It was a good lesson to me on how to get along and how not to get along with the Congress.

A word about delegating authority. It applies to both military and civilian 'commands,' but probably it is more expected of you in the former. Delegating authority extends your effectiveness. Your authority is felt in wider circles, or, in organizational chart terms, both vertically and horizontally. As a military commander or a civilian chief executive officer you would be little more than a figurehead if you decided to do everything yourself. It would be like trying to get a B-17 off the ground alone.

On the other hand, the more you assign specific responsiblities to capable people, the more you get done. The effect is cybernetic. A team takes over. The accomplishments of the whole become greater than that of the sum of its individual parts.

A few points to observe along the way:

Know your people.

Demand strict accountablity.

Give credit where credit is due.

How does one know whether a person is worthy of being given additional responsibility? When I was in charge of Air Materiel Command, I decided to check on the educational background of my top officers, mostly Generals with a few Colonels. Here is what I found. One officer had been at the head of his class. All of the others had been in the bottom quarter.

What this meant to me was that getting others to follow and to put in hard work had nothing necessarily to do with high scholastic grades. It had much more to do with integrity, loyalty, and leadership qualities. That is the kind of person I looked for to head a Division or spark an activity. They never fail you in either the military or business world.

This conclusion is not anti-education. It is pro-work. I am, as you know, an ardent supporter of higher education both in and out of the military. Early in my military career, when I was assigned to the Administrative Branch of the Field Service Section at Wright-Patterson, my boss was Major Benny Meyers. He was very smart. I learned much from him. He had improved himself by attending Babson Institute.

Hard workers who never let you down can be identified. Give a person hard work and see if he lets you down. But it is not always possible to make such a scientific test. More often than not , you have to delegate specific authority on a gut feeling and on general impression.

As an outdoorsman, I have found that a man's true character comes to light on a fishing or hunting trip. By chatting with them while waiting for the pickerel to bite, or exchanging views while waiting for ducks to show, I sense their philosophy, their inner nature. The men I have selected in this way have never failed me and have turned out to be valuable human resources.

Demanding strict accountability is a lot more mechanical. Periodic reports in person or in writing comprise the main tools for accountability. But the periods you set are to be the outside limits, not inside limits. Each person to whom you delegate authority must have easy access to you so that you can be promptly informed of any developments, negative or positive. Wherever possible, I maintained an open door policy. It has many advantages, and as a catalyst to accountability, recommend it.

At the start of this book there is a page devoted to acknowledgements — giving credit to those who have played a special role in my professional life. It is an author's way of giving credit where credit is due. I find it a rather paltry way to do it. I would rather give a testimonial dinner to each. I would rather shake his hand, look him

Future Military Management

in the eye, and hand him a plaque or citation. People deserve recognition for a job well done. It is not a matter of ego satisfaction. It is a matter of spiritual satisfaction. We are all here to help make this a better world. It is difficult to see the change yourself, so when your colleagues affirm that you have made a change, you get an indescribable satisfaction that transcends money.

And you are ready for the next challenge.

So much for the delegation of authority. Now a word about your own exercise of authority.

Authority is like the biblical loaves and fishes. You can delegate and delegate and delegate, but it is still all there. You can never relieve yourself of the ultimate responsibility. This means you cannot take refuge in an ivory tower. You have to get out from behind that desk and work eyeball to eyeball with people.

One morning, when I was stationed at Wright-Patterson, an officer named Ed asked if I would co-pilot for him as he tested a Consolidated B-24 bomber. I agreed. We loaded up on the ramp and revved up the motors.

Ed called to me, "Release the flap control."

I pulled the lever to do that as we began our roll. But the flaps did not respond.

"Flaps! Flaps!" he yelled.

I wrestled with the lever to no avail. For some reason the flaps did not retract, giving us too much air resistance. Ed put on full power, with the manifold pressure all the way to the red line. We hung to the runway. I saw the low hill at the end of the runway racing toward us.

At the last moment, we broke ground. Now the landing gear would not retract, giving us added resistance. We rose ten or fifteen feet, just enough to clear the hill. Ed made a slow turn, came around and landed. We taxied to the hanger where mechanics could check over the controls.

But we did not await the outcome. We were both shaking from the ordeal. We drove home and had a good stiff drink.

That close call was memorable because it was unnecessary. It need not have happened. If the officer in charge of that maintenance had personally inspected the work of the mechanics, the problem with the wing flaps and the landing gear could have been corrected before instead of after.

The 'after' could have been a lot worse. Such is the life of a flyer.

Control of Air Force operations has multiplied in complexity with each technological advance. As we no longer fly aircraft by "the seat of our pants," neither can we guide the operation of the Air Force by personal touch.

Personal touch — the hallmark of my own double careers — is not always as applicable as one may like.

Statistical information is gathered at all levels and at all geographical points and made available to the echelons that need it — at a push of a button. This information becomes a personnel information system, providing data on personnel strength and individual assignments, promotions, transfers, etc. It also becomes a Combat Operations Reporting System, able to supply data needed to determine the adequacy of combat fire readiness and performance.

In order to extend the personal touch despite the impersonal nature of data processing, we sampled even the attitudes of airmen, at least in my day. What was his attitude toward continuing; that is, making a career out of the Air Force? How did he feel about his housing conditions, job performance, treatment? By learning his opinion we could root out the causes of dissatisfaction and keep morale high.

An example of the wartime effectiveness of statistical systems was the Korean hostilities. Within four days after action commenced, combat readiness and combat operation statistics were flowing to the staff daily. Within seven days logistical summaries were available.

The military and the industrial are delicate balances in the use of raw materials, tools, facilities — and people. Data processing and a modern accounting system, from top to bottom, far advanced from the one we started in the late forties, are no longer merely recommended. They are a required way of life not only in the control of funds but in enabling commanders to make solid program and operating decisions.

Psychologists are currently dividing people into type A or type B personalities for the purpose of determining their susceptibility to certain mental illnesses. Military people are also divisible into two groups for the purpose of determining their dependability. Group A are those who constantly look for ways to avoid duties and responsibility. The goldbrickers. Group B are those who handle duties and responsiblities and thrive on accomplishment. They are the ones who

Future Military Management

are willing to go that extra mile.

The country needs Group B. Group A are the losers. Group B are the winners.

****

In the winter of 1934-35 there were rumblings of trouble with the civilian airmail carriers. President Roosevelt cancelled all government airmail contracts that March and turned the task over to U.S. Army Air Corps. Elements of the 12th Observation Group at Brooks Field, Texas, had been attached to Headquarters of the Central Division in Chicago in preparation for such an event.

In February I flew an open cockpit 019 north to Chicago. I was soon assigned to the mail route between Chicago and Omaha, and by early March was making that run in the bitter cold. I wore the heaviest flying suit I could find, but that bitter cold still got to me. To make matters worse, we flew mostly at night. We had no radio, so had to rely on light beacons located every forty or fifty miles.

An occasional snow squall hid those beacons from view. One member of my squadron flew into a hillside during such a squall and was killed. Two other planes were fortunate enough to be able to make emergency landings. Actually, the only instruments we had in those days were compass, air speed indicator, and turn and bank indicator.

This was not the work for which we joined the Air Corps. We were risking our lives, not for the country, but for the mail. Still, I did not hear any grumbling. We did what we had to do. We went that extra mile. The postal mess was cleaned up in late March and I was glad to get back to Texas.

Something good often comes of something bad. Well, the Air Corps flying the mail was not good. But it pointed out the lack of good radios, first rate instruments and the absence of closed cockpits. As a result, Congress passed appropriations that provided, in due time, all of the above.

The work ethic in the United States today is not as alive and well as it once was. During World War I, when I was 13, it was impossible for farmers to get help. Everyone old enough and physically fit was in the military service. My two great-uncles, Henry and Charlie Nelson, owned a threshing rig. Because of the lack of help, they had to resort to stack threshing; that way they could get by with one man on each stack. Uncle Henry would start the engine and pitch from one stack; I would pitch from the other. Uncle Charlie would adjust the separator.

It was hard work. But about 10 A.M. and again at 3 P.M. the wives would bring out cake, cookies, coffee, and lemonade. What a treat to look forward to! It was also fun to see the fruits of our labor; golden grain flowing into the wagon. And it was fun to get some pocket money.

Looking back at this now, I learned a lot about the gratification side of hard work. Today most youngsters frown on hard work. They see it as drudgery, not fun. Perhaps it was used as punishment once. Whatever the cause, they see hard work as something to be avoided. If they want to become strong — as I did threshing wheat — they use barbells. When these youngsters arrive in the military or in business, what kind of productivity do you think we can expect of them? Work ethic needs to be taught to our youngsters at an early age.

Although I do not have access to specific facts and figures at this time to collaborate what I am about to say, it appears that military procurement is not as cost efficient as it once was. Much of the difficulty is attributable to cost-plus contracts. These are necessary where contractors are treading on unknown ground. The government needs to protect the contractors from loss due to unexpected costs. However, the contractors should be made to protect the government by providing cost information extending down into subcontractors and, if necessary, sub-subcontractors. Cost-plus contracts in any field aim to protect the seller from jeopardy, but the buyer deserves that protection, too, especially if it's taxpayers' money.

The public has an interest in military expenditures, and, consequently, so does Congress. The military dares not risk losing the confidence of the public or of Congress. We should be relentless in our efforts toward maintaining public and Congressional confidence in the integrity of the military and its ability to manage its affairs on sound business principles.

A word about liquor. I admire a man who can hold his liquor, but I have little respect for the man who overdoes it. Who does not also deplore the increasing problem with drugs? Every officer in the

Future Military Management

military needs to be alert to both of these threats from within, exerting total onslaught against any sign of drugs, and total concern over the abuse of alcohol.

I was stationed in Honolulu in 1930, during Prohibition. Everybody had his own bootlegger and thought his was the best. Ours used to make delivery on his motorcycle. We would go to him and get a five gallon oaken keg filled and bring it back into the bathroom. There we would place it next to the commode, on its side. Anybody going to the john was required to roll the keg. This caused the aging process to progress more rapidly. We had the mellowest "Okolehao" around. Looking back on it now, I suppose we thought we were using it with discretion and under control.

Military training is both physical and technical. The navigator, radio operator, and pilot must not only be skilled in their job, but they must be trained to build the physical stamina needed in time of combat.

I would like to blow the horn in favor of a third factor. Everybody needs to be trained in business. Management is not the sole responsibility of the military Comptroller. Management in the military is everybody's business. It must be incorporated into our thinking, our training, our everyday activities. It must start at the lowest echelons and extend to the top.

We must be relentless in our determination to find easier, better, and more economical ways of doing things. We must continue to find new ideas and more effective methods for improving our business operations. We must instill in the minds of all of our people, in every branch of the service and in every endeavor, a cost consciousness, an ability to balance resources, a preference for mind power over manpower, and a continuing awareness of the public's interest in the sound use of military dollars.

A group of civilians made an interesting comment on the similarities of military and civilian problems. The occasion was the final regular meeting of the General Mills Board of Directors prior to my departure. It read, in part, as follows:

"...From flying cadet to Four Star General, Ed Rawlings served his country with uncommon distinction, both in the air and at his desk. For eight years, as head of the Air Materiel Command, he directed with rare skill an organization of incredible size and bewildering complexity, earning thereby a reputation as the outstanding business management expert in the Armed Forces.

"What Ed Rawlings had learned was what General Mills needed in 1959; his strong leadership during the decade of the 1960s was the prime force in the dramatic transformation of our company to a size and a strength and diversity that far exceeded the highest expectations of those who had gone before..."

Here is a group of businessmen saying that what I had acquired in the military was exactly what a non-military corporation needed. To emphasize that theme, albeit in Air Force terminology, they said: "Ed Rawlings piloted General Mills into the jet stream of American industry, and when, in 1969, he turned the executive controls over to others, he had set us on a course that would serve us well far into the future."

This says more eloquently than can I that the two careers which I enjoyed may not have been as separate as they appeared. The two hats that I wore, first the military then the civilian, may have looked quite different, but really covered the same head.

The common denominator of any discipline in the pursuit of success is the human person.

All of which is really saying that everything in this chapter about my recommendations for the military also applies in principle to business.

Chapter XV

Better Business

In October, 1986, my class at Harvard Business School celebrated its 47½-year reunion at the Broadmoor Hotel in Colorado Springs. It included a visit to nearby U.S. Air Force Academy for a cadet review, lunch with the Superintendent, and the Navy-Air Force football game. You can probably guess who was the chairman in charge of arrangements. At an earlier reunion I was named the outstanding graduate of the Class of 1939. Now, helping with arrangements was the least I could do.

Each reunion with that class has strengthened my respect for the teaching methods at Harvard's Business School. I consider one of the keystones of that program the case study. As a student I hated the case study to start with. How could the professors expect a neophyte to understand a real business problem that was so complex even the experienced businessmen involved had a hard time solving it, if they could.

But that is the beauty of the case study teaching method. It is not so much book learning as it is real-life learning. You are thrown into these horrendous business situations and you have to swim. So you do.

At school I solved case study after case study. Then later, out in real life, it was no more real than the reality of my learning. And that was true for the Comptroller's Office, Air Materiel Command,

and General Mills.

Those reunions also confirm to me that everybody, no matter what direction his life takes, benefits by that Harvard program. Each alumnus radiates competence, and their business records reflect that competence.

So I start this chapter on business principles that pay off, by extolling Harvard Business School as a sound investment for anyone embarking on a business career.

Although I was not in full control of the exact time that I would attend Harvard's graduate business program, coming as it did a few years prior to our entering World War II turned out to be perfect timing. The skills I learned became critical to the Air Corps and then the Air Force.

Most of the time, we are in control of timing. In business, timing can be critical, so we must exercise that timing skill. It is perhaps more obvious in the military, where battles or war can be lost as a result of timing.

The Japanese strike on Pearl Harbor was perfectly timed. The attack involved so many aircraft and so many surprise and strategy factors that poor timing could have resulted in collisions, not to mention loss of surprise and effectiveness. An example of poor timing was the collision of a Dutch aircraft with a Pan American plane on a Canary Island runway in which some 500 passengers were killed. A minute or two could have prevented that catastrophe.

In business, some products are ahead of their time. Marketing men wonder why their exceptional product lays an egg. Later, a similar product offered by the competition sells. Other products are behind the times. Marketing men try to jump aboard the bandwagon only to find it has turned into a hearse.

The basic approach to proper timing is in market research. However, if the elapsed time from the completion of that research to the delivery of the product to the consumer is excessive, you run the risk of "missing the boat."

This is another instance where sound military logistics is also sound business practice. By shortening your production, delivery, and distribution times, you not only cut down on costs, but lower your risk of poor timing.

The old time and motion studies that led to more accurate cost

At War

accounting methods decades ago are still valid in principle. If wasted motion is leading to a loss of time, correcting that motion can lead to a gain in profits.

We are all conscious. If we don't punch clocks, we meet quotas based on time and we base our profit and loss statements on time periods. These are months, quarters, and years. But what about minutes, hours, days, and weeks? Our consciousness of time should be focused to make us more aware of the importance of these smaller periods.

We need to arrive early — worker or executive — and we need to set periodic goals during the day that keep us on a time target. If a person is prompt and keeps his appointments, chances are he will do everything on time and be a more dependable and productive person.

Punctuality is its own reward. Prizes and bonuses may be in order for sales competitions and the like, but there is no need to reward a person for being at his desk on time. The reward comes with the satisfaction of doing a job well.

On a military inspection trip to Europe with four or five of my staff, we finished in France near Paris and decided to go to the Follies Bergere. I got tired at 2 A.M. and told the others they could stay all night if they wished, but we were going to take off for Germany at 7 A.M. That morning I was on deck at 6:50 A.M. along with the plane's crew but no staff members. I told the crew to warm up the plane. At 7 o'clock none of the staff had arrived and I climbed aboard. I gave them five more minutes. Then we took off for Germany. They caught up with me four days later. We had no more tardiness after that.

Good timing requires an executive to keep informed. This information gathering must go beyond the news media. It must tap both the microcosm and macrocosm of the business world.

If I needed information at General Mills about internal matters, the company dining room was frequently a good source. Also, General Mills was close enough to Minneapolis to go to the Minneapolis Club for lunch. Here I could meet business leaders of the city and get a bit wider perspective. As head of a milling company, I was entitled to sit at the Millers' table. I had great discussions with the millers about business affairs of the day and goings-on in the city.

I still keep in touch with the friends I made at that table, especially Bill Lohman, former national flour sales manager for General Mills, whom I can call whenever I want the latest Twin Cities news.

On a larger scale, you can employ the services of information-gathering companies that operate on a national scale and go forward and backward in time. They can give you a record of some past business effort, survey the present, and hold a mirror up to the future. We used such a firm, as I have already related, prior to our decision to close a number of flour mills. Their evaluation of the future of flour milling for bakers supported our own opinion and gave us the reinforcement we needed to proceed with a major divestiture at General Mills, for which nobody there has ever been sorry.

There are a number of forecast services to which an executive can subscribe. I happen to like Elliot Janeway, a political economist, of New York — about 95 percent of the time accurate, I believe. This accuracy is attributable to the quality of his own sources, as it would be for any forecast service. He appears to tap both sides of the political aisle and rely on solid government contacts. But then this is a personal choice; each executive must make the selection based on his or her own requirements.

A word about new ideas. (A word is not really enough; they really deserve their own book.) New ideas are what a company needs to stay on the profit side. New ideas are what a country needs to survive political and trade competition.

If their timing is right and they fulfill a solid need, new ideas are the catalyst of increased sales. That's the good news. Not the bad news. Many a new idea has been buried by bureaucratic resistance and corporate inertia.

A company climate has to be amenable to new ideas. The I-did-not-think-of-it syndrome which snuffs out most support must be replaced by a more company-wide philosophy of "what is good for the company is good for me."

Once born, a new idea needs to be nurtured with patience. Of course, the chief nurturer is its originator. He or she must be emotionally committed to the brainchild and be able to enlist the understanding of its value from others. And these others must realize that, just because the originator is a high school dropout and not a distinguished scientist, does not necessarily reflect on the ultimate value

At War

of the new idea.

A new idea was born to me one rainy morning while I was fishing. I was wearing special rain gear. I had to relieve myself and saw there was no fly, so I had to remove the rain gear and get soaked while taking care of my needs. You can bet that when I got home, I sent a simple design to the company that would allow for such a contingency. Necessity is indeed the mother of invention.

We are all potential creators. Creativity knows no human barrier. I have seen secretaries come up with excellent ideas. Even a board chairman might come up with a good idea!

I'm glad I mentioned secretaries. During my military and business careers, I have had about ten secretaries, and every one of them has been good. I recall worrying every time I was faced with a change. Would my new secretary be as good as my present secretary? More often than not the new secretary was every bit as efficient.

We employers underrate secretaries. Generally, they are capable of doing more involved things than we are willing to assign to them. My advice to a young executive is to rely more on your secretary.

Consult your secretary when you buy computer hardware or software or when you install new office phones or systems. Introduce her to visitors in your office. Treat her less as a subordinate, more as a colleague. Give her credit when it is due. Be as understanding about her needs as she is about yours. In other words, treating a secretary in a way that puts her up instead of puts her down enables her to perform for you in a higher capacity.

Manpower and womanpower are the most important ingredients in any operation. Put the right person in the right spot and you will have clearer sailing. If a quarter of the players in a show are miscast, you've got a flop. A business is even more sensitive to people power. The wrong person in the wrong job only ten percent of the time can mean a five percent loss instead of a five percent profit.

Education is good. Top of the class is good. But somebody who engenders enthusiasm in others is better. And somebody with special capabilities to do a special job is better still.

Small businesses have different problems than large businesses. The family of a mom and pop retail store have to be their own secretary, sales force, and production line. They have to wash their own windows, sweep their own floors, do their own advertising (usually a handwritten sign in the window) and conduct their own market surveys.

I grew up in such a family. My uncle and father were partners in a hardware store, and they were their own boss. They had to make it on their own or not at all.

Today, small business firms are the heart pulse of America. But small has become larger. And large has become a conglomerate. There is a natural advantage to size. Fixed costs can be spread over a wider base. You can afford professional skills, technical equipment, and the right person for the right job.

But size also brings larger responsibilities. Take General Mills. It is committed to competitive excellence. It strives to maintain leadership among consumer goods companies through a strategy of balanced diversification, aggressive consumer marketing, and sound positioning within each industry group. Its size, however, requires that it also be committed to good corporate "citizenship." It must endeavor to be responsible and anticipatory in serving its primary constituencies. That means shareholders, consumers, employees, and even society in general.

Yes, big companies must watch their earnings per share, their percentage return on equity, and their share of the total market. But they must also watch their labor market, their labor turnover, and their labor standard of living.

The figures on financial statements are made by human figures. People are the key assets in any company. Where labor unions represent those people, we at General Mills made every effort to keep those unions informed of our activities, both problems and solutions. As a result, we minimized the adversarial relationship that seems traditional in the United States between labor and management. Wherever this polarization occurs, it is costly to both sides. I vote for less confrontation and more cooperation in labor-management relations.

Complexities of big business far exceed my ability to boil them down to some simple all-encompassing principle like "there's no free lunch." All one can do is use the brains and experience of the people on the team to maximum benefit.

On this score, I recommended to George Weyerhaeuser, chief executive officer of the company that bears his name, that he should bring back his retired executives once a year — all expenses paid,

At War

including those of the spouse — and let them sit in on the annual stockholder meeting and board meeting. If they had any comments or input they could write it out and turn it in or participate orally, but they could not vote.

Weyerhaeuser agreed, and at this time (April 1987) I have just returned from their annual meeting where a few other retired directors were also in attendance. I believe some of the comments were well received and bore the hallmarks of wisdom and experience that are hard to buy.

I have made this same proposal to General Mills and it does so for stockholder meetings, but not for board meetings.

In order to broaden the concept's exposure to other companies, I wrote an article for Harvard Business Review elaborating on the advantages of keeping their senior directors on top in this way. It did not get published as an article, but the Review did publish it as a letter to the editor. A magazine published by a large executive recruitment agency, Waybill, has quoted my Harvard letter in detail, giving it more exposure.

Talent is where you find it. But just the way the bluebird was found, after a wide-flung search, to be residing in the searcher's own backyard, so can talent be in your own company. A talent search can be more thorough and precise inside than it can be outside a company. As attractive as an available outside executive might seem, there are immeasurables and unknowns about him. Similarly, to him there are immeasureables and unknowns about you. These mutual uncertainties are not likely to exist to any degree with an inside man. Take 1984 as an example. It is interesting that 60 percent of the executives involved in organizational changes in General Mills were people already with the company. The highest percentage was found in the Consumer Foods division; other divisions gave greater emphasis to college recruiting and to identifying other sources of talent when the need arose.

Some men ought to retire before they reach 65. They are doddering before their time. But, many have plenty of go-to-it-iveness in them at 70, 75, and older. With productivity on the decline, what company can afford to scrap the potential for increased productivity these business solutions can provide? And how about their potential as ambassadors of goodwill at stockbrokers meetings? A company could have no better rooter than a retired director.

The difference between an executive who ages before his years and the executive who remains productive beyond his years is: stress. We need to protect our manpower from this killer to whatever extent we can. It is not always possible to provide a stress-insulated environment, but the least we can do is provide health and/or recreational facilities for use in non-working hours.

Very soon after I took over the presidency of General Mills, I had a health club built in the basement of the headquarters building. It housed steam baths, exercise equipment, a massage room, and showers. The man we put in charge was an excellent masseur. If an executive felt pressure and went down to the health club, he sure felt like a new man when he returned to his desk, and that included me.

However, I enjoyed more relief from stress over the weekends. There's nothing like hunting or fishing to make you forget faltering sales, new competitive products, and heavy promotional expenditures. Before we bought and improved Wondra, our General Mills camp in Northern Minnesota, I used to find a trip down to Alton Raney's duck camp in Arkansas a perfect relief from stress. I got to know the place while in the military, inviting Nate Twining and others to join me. Later, General Mills people, like Bill Lang and Charlie Bell, enjoyed the fun there.

Large companies should sponsor trips or acquire facilities to give the average worker a chance to recharge in natural environments. The great outdoors keeps one young.

A time saver, and therefore at least partially a stress saver, for executives who travel a lot is the company plane. This is often considered an extravagance. One of the many conditions that Iacocca had to comply with to get a federal loan guarantee was to sell the Chrysler jets. This was a false economy. Commercial flying may be cheaper if a man's time is worth little, but for executives on the go, a company plane saves a lot of cooling your heels.

Recently the press reported that Hemmeter Corporation, based in Hawaii, had purchased a Boeing 727. Chris Hemmeter explained that the jet's 4,200-mile range would enable him and his staff to fly to any of the company's resort building projects planned for Osaka, Hong Kong, Australia, Aruba, and Florida. A private office, three large work tables, and twenty-one reclining seats would enable the

At War

staff to continue working as if they were in their office. In addition, there was space for such cargo on these flights as special marble or fixtures. The estimate given on flight time was 400 to 500 hours a year. Even when you figure the cost of a specially-trained captain, first officer, and flight engineer, that place can be a money-saver.

Such a plane probably cost about $7 million. The cost needs to be evaluated against the savings. If the company does not have the cash, then the cost of borrowing must be taken into consideration in calculating the total cost. But then, in evaluating the savings, you need to figure the added work hours this mode of travel makes possible. If a company does not have its own plane, yet is located near a private airport, it might want to look into the feasibility of buying or leasing a jet.

We need to take care of our people's peace of mind with health care insurance and life insurance. The cost appears in black and white each year and may tend to obscure the balancing advantages which are not as concrete. But these advantages are there, hidden in lowered per unit costs: peace of mind produces better attendance and productivity.

Inside every nonproductive person is a person with a problem. It could be a problem at home or a problem at work. The problems at home can be sensed by the personnel manager and once identified can be handled through appropriate counseling.

The problems at work cannot easily be identified by personnel people. These are production problems that are the domain of managers, foremen, and executives.

Firing somebody is a painful job. You could be causing a man and his family a traumatic experience from which they may never recover. And it may be unnecessary; the man might just be in the wrong slot.

Whether military or business, the employee has been well screened or he would not be there at all. The employer could be at fault, not the employee. Sometimes a contractor or supplier of materials or equipment involved in the employee's work can be of assistance in identifying the problem. They know the skills involved and can better evaluate the person's skills to see if they dovetail. Before discharging a person, consider trying that person in another job.

Discharge is costly. It costs your company. It costs the discharged worker. It costs the community. It costs the country. It is a solution only of last resort.

I could go on for pages on business decisions, on inventories, on acquisitions, on taxes on the national debt, and on the international trade imbalance. But I won't.

I prefer closing this business chapter with a tribute to the American worker. He is an asset no business can survive without. This asset should be protected and nurtured.

The American male and the American female are loyal, adventuresome, creative, and resourceful. They respond when called upon. They rise to challenges. They personify the American spirit. A company that gives them their due receives more than fairness in return. That company is the beneficiary of the hard work, integrity, and devotion to duty that has built our nation.

I owe my success to people.

Chapter XVI

Into the Future

January 23, 1983, was the saddest day of my life. On that day I lost my beloved wife Pete. She had been at my side for over fifty years. I was devastated and alone.

But I was not alone for long. When the tragic news reached my sons, they and their wives rushed to be with me. I was overwhelmed by the love and support shown by my family and many friends.

For the last ten years of her life, Pete had suffered with arthritis. Fortunately, it did not affect her hands. She was able to keep up with her painting and did some beautiful work in this period. But at times the crippling effect of the arthritis was so bad, it kept her confined to a wheelchair. I was grateful it did not adversely affect her spirit. She remained cheerful, active, and creative. But she was not able to get any real exercise and it was to this lack of exercise that the doctors attributed the fatal clot.

* * * *

I was fortunate to have my two granddaughters, Kelly and Wendy Rawlings, attending Hamline University in St. Paul. They spent many weekends with me and they really cheered me up. We had fun together, I got my skates out and we skated on Lake Minnetonka.

Of course, there was the hard work of first sweeping the snow off the ice. In the spring when the weather turned warm we would go swimming together. My dog, Brownie, a handsome Chesapeake Bay retriever, would join us in the water. I think I have tried hard to spoil my grandchildren, but they seem to be the kind of young people that are strong, independent, and — unspoilable.

Even though my four sons and their families have been geographically scattered, they managed to get together on the shores of Lake Minnetonka for our 40th and 50th wedding anniversaries in 1970 and 1980.

Now we decided to get the family together again a couple of years later for my 80th birthday. My son, Peter, and I wanted to do it up right, so many more people were invited.

Then somebody asked me if I was certain that it was my 80th. I stopped to figure it out. Lo and behold! It was really only my 79th. Plans were so far along, we decided to go ahead. Everybody had a great time. Then, the following year, I was able to have a second 80th birthday celebration.

Now it was 1984 and a gala event took place at our house and the Yacht Club in Excelsior, Minnesota. It was like "This Is Your Life," except for the element of surprise. I knew there would be a boat ride on the *Lady of the Lake,* a paddle steamer, with cocktails and entertainment. Yes, I knew dinner would be served at 7 P.M. followed by my blowing out the candles and cutting of the cake. I had an idea which key people would be there. Jim Fish, former head of advertising at General Mills and now a professor at St. Thomas College, read a "This Is Your Life" script telling of my childhood, even of the windmill I climbed. He related my attempted enlistment at age 13; my receiving the Dr. Workman award upon graduation from high school for being the outstanding student-athlete; my purchase of the double barrel shotgun for $1.50; my sharpshooter award and how I shot eleven birds with ten shots.

Talk about telling tales out of school, somebody really did the homework on my boyhood days: my first jobs, picking mustard for fifteen cents an hour, milking cows, and shovelling snow off the sidewalks.

Dr. Graham, president of Hamline, was there. Also, a classmate of mine at Hamline, Virginia Taylor, had flown in from Kenosha,

Into the Future

Wisconsin. I sat there wondering what was going to happen next as they told about how seeing Lindbergh inspired me; how I decided to become a reservist; and how the Dayton Company tried to talk me out of resigning but finally accepted it. Richard Schall of the Dayton Company was asked to stand.

When the account of my life reached my stint in Hawaii, they gave the spotlight to my late wife, and there were my sister-in-law Dora Peterson and her son Skip, who had flown in from Hawaii. Asked to stand up were my sons and their wives: Col. Peter and his wife, Beverly, all the way from Virginia; John and Sally, then of Steamboat Springs, Colorado; and Dick and Barbara of Shorewood, Minnesota. Granddaughters Wendy and Kelly, were also asked, to stand. My son Gerry, and his wife, Kathy, missed the dinner because of business. Absent, too, were six other grandchildren.

"General, do you remember how the engine of your 019 coughed and flames engulfed the cockpit, burning the skin on your right hand and nose? You went over the side and pulled the ring of your chute. Little did you know then that, more than fifty years later, you would be the principal speaker at the national convention of the Caterpillar Clubs."

I relived that jump. Listening, I relived my first experiences with IBM punch cards in Dayton, my Harvard Business School days, the prewar aircraft build-up, wartime logistics, postwar readjustment, and my appointment as first Comptroller of the Air Force.

When the narration told how General Spaatz decorated me with the Distinguished Service medal, General Curtis LeMay and General Bozo McKee stood up to be recognized.

Then came my years as head of Air Materiel Command, making full General, my military retirement, and my appointment to General Mills.

My eyes watered. Maybe it was the smoke in the room. Or maybe it was the love being expressed to me by all who were present. Here it gets blurred. Divesting General Mills of its feed division and closing many of its mills...the growth of profits...a Tennessee Ernie Ford tape...my General Mills retirement dinner...Charlie Bell and James McFarland stood...my work with computer literacy programs...Air Force Academy.

Jim Fish left the podium. Everybody stood and sang "Happy

Birthday."

It was my turn to stand. I stood and surveyed those wonderful friends and colleagues. Then I bowed my head in tribute to them. As I recall, there were over 150 people at the dinner. I appreciated the tribute they had shown me because many had traveled a long way — Mr. and Mrs. Mort Wilner had flown in from Washington, D.C.; Elliot Janeway came from New York; General and Mrs. Leo Dahl came from Alabama; John Parker came from Washington, D.C.; Gerry and Mrs. LeMay came from Newport Beach, California. Three of my four sons and their wives, my sister and her husband, two granddaughters, my sister-in law and her son, all made trips to share this happy time. Mrs. Gresty, who is Sally Rawlings's mother, came from San Diego. Bless them all.

* * * *

I had been making occasional visits to Honolulu. I loved Hawaii and intended one day to sell the Lake Minnetonka house and at least winter in Hawaii. On one of those visits, my first winter in Honolulu, I met Kathryn Fradkin. Kathryn had not only been raised in Minnesota, she maintained a summer home up in the lake country even though she married shortly after graduating from the University of Minnesota and lived in New York most of her adult life. A friend of mine from Washington, D.C., Mike, was spending some time in Honolulu during the winter of 1986.

Mike had lost his wife a few years before, but he told me about how a friend, Mary, had brought so much happiness into his life. At breakfast at the Royal I asked Mike, "Why don't you and Mary get married?"

He replied, "Neither one of us want to get married."

That afternoon Kathy and I were visiting out on the lanai, and I told her of Mike's remarks. We feel into a dead silence, said nothing, but I now realize silence sometimes is golden. We had both realized that we each had a good life, were financially secure, had travel and friends galore. However, the companionship we gave each other truly embellished both our lives. We realized we were good to, and for each other. The date was set, October 10, 1986.

We sent out the invitations. The ceremony was to be at the beau-

Into the Future

tiful Air Force Academy Chapel in Colorado Springs. A note attached to the invitations read, "Since we have an ample supply of crystal, silver, china, and ducks, we request no gifts. However, should you wish to make a contribution, do so to the Falcon Foundation, Air Force Academy. Tax exempt." Several thousand dollars in contributions were made to the Foundation.

October 10th was a most exciting day. I left the Broadmoor at 6 A.M. for a Board Meeting of the Falcon Foundation. Kathy was sharing a suite with my wonderful secretary, Janet Svendson. I left word at the desk to have calls directed to their suite. Gordon Reed, his son, Thomas, and Jake Saleba reached Kathy and explained they wanted to see me. They suggested she come down and join them for lunch.

Kathy left word with the doorman to direct me into the dining room as soon as I arrived at the hotel. Somehow I slipped by the doorman. Kathy, feeling I should be back, called my room, "Gordon Reed and Jake Saleba want to have a visit with you."

I was as anxious to see them as they were to see me and said, "Bring them right up."

They were flying out right after the wedding. Kathy told how Gordon asked Jake, "Would you fly all the way from the East coast to attend a wedding, and not even be able to attend the champagne reception.?"

Jake answered, "No, I wouldn't do it for any other man in the world, but nothing could keep me away from the wedding and getting to see that wonderful friend of mine again." We were having a wonderful visit when Kathy looked at her watch and exclaimed, "It is a quarter of three and we have to get dressed and drive twenty miles out to the Academy!" Kathy claims she never got dressed in such a hurry.

My driver, Bernie, had the car right in front of the hotel, motor going. "Step on it," I said to Bernie. "Don't worry about speeding tickets. Just get us to the church on time!"

Meanwhile, at the Chapel, family and guests had arrived. The organ was playing. The only things missing were the bride and groom. General Curtis LeMay looked at his watch nervously. He had agreed to coordinate the event, and now it looked like his efforts were to go down the drain. Had we changed our minds?

Rawlings

Just as he was about to make the announcement that would send everyone back home wondering, we arrived at the rear of the chapel. It was a beautiful ceremony. There is probably no more exquisite chapel in the world. Kathy and I will never forget that day.

* * * *

I finally sold the house on Lake Minnetonka. I had Pete's ashes moved to the Air Academy Cemetery in Colorado Springs, where I would be able to pay an occasional visit. Kathy and I decided to summer in 1987 in Steamboat Springs and to winter in Honolulu for six months.

We have a condominium a couple of blocks from the ocean. I do not enjoy ocean fishing, so I wait for the months in Colorado for that. But I do enjoy hunting game in Hawaii. Both the islands of Molokai and Kauai are great for partridge and golden plover. My office is just a block from our condo. And there is plenty going on there.

One of my favorite spots in Honolulu is the Royal Hawaiian Hotel. I have a table with a black walnut, four-star plaque bearing the names "Thacker-Rawlings" where we have breakfast every morning. Often we have notable persons with us. For example, recently I had Max Winter, owner of the Minnesota Vikings football team.

Not only do I enjoy having breakfast at the Royal every morning, but Kathy and I enjoy going there in the evening to be entertained by Carmen and Keith Haugen. Carmen is a most attractive Hawaiian girl from Maui. Keith was born in Greenbush, Minnesota. They are a most gifted couple and we have come to think of them as special friends. Keith plays the guitar and sings, Carmen plays the ukelele and sings. Carmen does a beautiful hula. She always makes it a point to do a special hula right at our table.

What goes on in my office?

The Computer Consortium, Air Force activities, management consultation, and charities make every day a busy one.

In recent years I have devoted time to the Civilian/Military Institute where I served as vice president and director. It is an organization dedicated to generating a better understanding between the State Department and top military officers of the relationship between our

Into the Future

foreign policy and our military posture. The Institute conducts symposia around the country to communicate the foreign policy/military strength relationship to business and other leaders.

As important as this activity is, I consider my work with the Boys Clubs of Honolulu just as important. I was first introduced to Boys Clubs shortly after joining General Mills. Jack Cornelius took me over to visit the Minneapolis Boys Club, located in the north part of the city where delinquency was the highest. After my orientation, I was invited to join the Club's board. I accepted.

During the first year of that Club's operation, the delinquency rate dropped 50 percent. I was convinced I had joined the right organization to help young people.

In those days we were making yearly treks to Pete's home in Honolulu to visit with her family. I had come to know some of Hawaii's leading citizens like Bill Quinn, former Governor and then President of Dole Pineapple; Earl Thacker, one of the largest realtors; and investment specialist Charley Spalding. Charley was President of the Honolulu Boys Club and when he asked me to join, I immediately said yes.

The Honolulu Boys Club had an effect similar to its Minneapolis counterpart: a large percent reduction in delinquency the first year of operation. Juvenile judges are the best supporters of these Clubs in both cities.

Did you ever witness a race involving handicapped youngsters? Talk about grit and drive. Here the human spirit is emblazoned in stark drama for all to admire. That is why I continue to support the Chileda Habilitation Institute, A LaCrosse, Wisconsin, based world-renowned home for multi-handicapped children. Again, it was Jack Cornelius, who along with John Lamb, first introduced me to this commendable activity. Jack, president emeritus of American Heritage Foundation; John, former president of the Minnesota Advertising Federation, and myself drove from Minneapolis down the river to LaCrosse, where Chileda is located. My driver, Sue, drove us down in my maroon Continental, and we discussed Chileda all the way. After viewing the facilities, but more importantly, watching the physical therapy and moral support that went with it, Jack and John asked in unison, "Ed is this an effort you can support? "Of course," I replied, ready to reach for my checkbook, "These kids deserve all the help we can give them." But," I continued, "don't you both agree that what we really need is a National Advisory Board?" Agreement was reached easily and quickly...ideas and thoughts flowed freely as we then and there determined to brainstorm the Advisory Board possibility on the trip back home.

So as Sue continued to drive us back up the mighty Mississippi, the Chileda National Advisory Board was born and being spanked into life in the back seat of my car. Before we got to Lake City, we had already nominated the first members. Prominent generals such as Mark Clark, and Russ Dougherty. Business leaders such as Justin Dart, Rhiney Reinhart, Russ Cleary, John L. Burns, Dr. Jake Stutzman, Mrs. Russ (Patricia) Lund, and Internationalists such as Mohammed Benjelloun, all were part of that first group. They didn't know it then but they were all involved. Just as, I thought, we were already involved. Was it physically possible? Then I remembered the indefatigable effort by a handicapped child to walk that I had just seen an hour or two earlier. The answer to the earlier question was to myself, as I spoke softly in a whisper, "Of course, I'll serve." Believe me, I was committed, and then some. But then so were all the others mentioned previously. Without exception they, along with the three of us, have served...are still serving on the Chileda National Advisory Board.

There is so much that needs to be done, one must be selective if one does not want to join the ranks of the destitute. I go by personal experience. There is hardly a day's mail that does not contain solicitations for worthy charities.

An example would be the Falcon Foundation. This is a support group for the United States Air Force Academy. How can I ever forget the break I received — a four-year scholarsip to Hamline University — while punting a football around an empty field one day. That education started me on my path. So many candidates for the U.S. Air Force Academy are stymied for financial reasons. Is this man to be deprived of generalship or that man deprived of statesmanship because of lack of tuition money? The least I could do was what others had done and were doing: donate enough money to create a scholarship.

The most important project one can assist is the project one originates. Computer usage is my baby.

Into the Future

When I was in command of AMC at Dayton, I had a bright young doctor working for me, Douglas Talbott. One day I asked him, "Doug, why scratch your head about symptoms; why not have a computer deliver the diagnosis?"

He laughed. "Would you like your family physician to be Dr. UNIVAC?"

"Maybe," I replied. "Dr. UNIVAC may be more reliable than some country doctors who have to be knowledgeable about latest treatments which they have not had the opportunity to learn. But I'm not suggesting computerized competition; I'm proposing computerized computation."

"Meaning..."

Now I knew I had his ear. "Meaning," I continued, "a computer is programmed with all of the physical symptoms and all of the illnesses they point to. A country doctor, with limited knowledge of some diseases and less on latest treatments, can dial into a central computer, give the illness symptoms, and get back the possible diseases and accepted treatments."

Dr. Talbott had a faraway look in his eyes. "A successful therapy that has not even appeared in the medical journals would be theirs to use!" Now I had more than his ear. I had his enthusiasm.

Our mutual enthusiasm was frustrated by money. We needed a backer. I approached "Boss" Kettering, one of the wealthiest men in America, who held some medically-oriented patents. What I did not know was that Kettering had no love for doctors. I got the short shrift.

Our great idea died aborning. At least, so it seemed. But something happened to Kettering that made him change his opinion of doctors, and he subsequently founded the Sloan-Kettering Institute in New York. And something happened in the medical profession: they discovered computers. Today, our idea is alive and well and is of invaluable help to the medical profession.

I remain committed to the Air Force on many fronts. These fronts were cited this year when, at the age of 82, I received the Air Force Exceptional Service Award. I was the youngest four-star general, and now maybe the oldest recipient of that Exceptional Service Award. I must be doing something right.

Activities cited in that Award were "support posts for the Air

Rawlings

Force Academy and as a booster and endower of scholarships to the Academy Preparatory School...sponsored numerous Aerospace Education Foundation Fellowships and played a large role in Air Force activities and recognition programs." I was really touched to receive this award from General Jack I. Gregory, Commander in Chief, Pacific Air Forces, at ceremonies at Hickam Air Force Base in March 1987.

Another honor came in 1981, when, in Minneapolis, the Ed Rawlings Chapter was established by a vote of the members of the Air Force Association. Today there are over 600 airmen in this squadron. What a thrill to have them flying in my name!

When I won the Air Force Exceptional Service Award in 1987, I was delighted to get a message of congratulations from the Chapter. It said, "Proud to have your name on our chapter banner." That goes double, fellows.

I remain committed to General Mills, and they to me. My office in Honolulu is an extension of my old office in Minneapolis. I walk to that office each morning, but I also may find it necessary to go there before or after office hours or on weekends to check some correspondence or write some reports.

General Mills Board Chairman and Chief Executive Officer H. Brewster Atwater, Jr., has my admiration for the fine job he is doing in piloting the company in what one might call turbulent air. Despite militant competition, he has led General Mills to new growth by providing consumers with products and services that are provably superior.

General Mills remains number one in the huge cereal market. They are number one in a variety of dessert and baking mix segments with Betty Crocker brownies, specialty cakes, frostings, pie crust mix, and premium muffins in the lead. Gold Medal flour remains number one, as does Bisquick. New acquisitions like Red Lobster Restaurants and Talbots have become clear market leaders.

Continual innovation and preemptive marketing are prerequisites to developing market leadership. Under Atwater, the company appears to have an energetic drive in this regard.

* * * *

Into the Future

Kathy recently had an accident which we can now say was a blessing in disguise. I was in Seattle and called her from the hotel. She was going to the phone when she tripped on a scatter rug, landing on a glass-top coffee table. She had to have six stitches in her head and had a black and blue area on her cheek. The next day our dependable girl Nineta couldn't come.

Here was Kathy without help, and I was on the other side of the Pacific. She did not tell me what had happened because she knew I had important appointments and was looking forward to spending the weekend with my son and his wife at their summer home just outside Seattle. We now refer to this accident as the "rude awakening" because it forced us to make a decision about our future.

I have appreciated that a part of the price of getting old is we may need to depend on others more and more, especially in physical emergencies such as Kathy's accident.

"Sweetie," I ventured, "this should teach us a lesson. If we are apart, somebody should always be with us."

"Yes," Kathy agreed, "but what about Steamboat?"

"Let's sell it. John and Sally are moving away from there to Seattle."

"Where will we go for the summer?"

"Air Force Village West."

Kathy threw up her hands. We had talked about that. "It's too regimented, Ed, do we really want an institution?"

"It's far from that," I insisted, "Look at this." We went over a brochure together, noting the full calendar of sound programs planned and the availability of recreational facilities at adjacent March Air Force Base. Maid service, a gourmet dining room, 24-hour security, San Bernadino and San Jacinto mountains providing breath-taking views and outdoor sports, and a fully-staffed health care center.

Kathy's interest perked up, and the more I sold her on it, the more enthused I became about the idea myself. The next day we made a commitment. We sold our Colorado summer house and now spend our summers in Air Force Village West at March Air Force Base.

I like living near an Air Force base. I can keep active and in touch with what I was born to do as well as be with air people. Gen. and Mrs. Curtis LeMay will be our neighbors there.

I like Hawaii, too. It will always be my winter home. It is always summer in Hawaii — a spring-like summer. A retired officer in Hawaii has many opportunities to enjoy military facilities, including golf, beaches, clubs, even the Hale Koa hotel, which was built with the profits generated from military installations. Hawaii enjoys the best of both worlds, military and civilian.

I remain committed to leadership, my own and others. It must be recognized, developed, and properly harnessed. My experience has been that hard workers generally make better leaders and executives.

"What did you do as a young person?" I often ask at an interview. I am looking for such answers as deliver papers, babysit, mow lawns, shovel snow, do odd jobs, and generally keep busy. these are the people who have developed a work ethic from an early age and are used to hard work.

Of course, I look for the other traits needed by a leader, too. Can the person communicate, win friends and influence people, set and reach goals, be flexible enough to adapt to specific situations, delegate, motivate, and organize?

And, when an executives fails, do they know how to pick themselves up, dust themselves off, and start up again? Education and religious leader, Paul H. Dunn, has been quoted as saying, "Success is not in never failing, but in rising every time you fail."

I am committed to making a difference. That is what we are here for.

Right now that committment, for one, is aimed at proliferating the use of computers in education. Hardly a week goes by when another college or university does not join the Computer Consortium — every one as a result of my personal effort.

Can you imagine that the majority of graduates receiving degrees these days do not know the meaning of micro-processor, diskette, or software? What is this going to do to America's competitive position in the international marketplace?

I am most disheartened to realize that we are no longer competitive in the world market. Take a look at our trade deficit. No, I am not worried about myself, nor my sons, but, I am worried about what the future holds for my grandchildren and great-grandchildren.

It is difficult to find clothing made in America, and I refuse to purchase what is made in Korea, Taiwan, or anywhere outside the

Into the Future
United States.

Japan is a classic example of a protected economy. They allow tobacco companies to sell American-made cigarettes in Japan, but their advertisements have to be in English. I think that we should make it a law that advertisements which appear in our newspapers, billboards, and media should be in the language of the country which produces the product.

Japan was originally known as the land of the "rising sun." It is now the land of the rising yen. I admire the diligence and hard work of other people, but I am first of all an American, and I say we must once again become competitive and turn our trade deficit around.

I have never driven a car that wasn't made in the United States, nor will I. We should wave the banner "Made in the United States." Union members refuse to go past a picket line. We might engage that same spirit to have them demand only products which bear the mark "Made in the United States." I don't care whether it is automobiles, cameras or clothing. Our country has the skill to turn out products equally as good as those made in Europe or the Oriental countries.

There was a surge of patriotism when the Statue of Liberty underwent a face-lift. Now, we should unveil the motto: "Buy products made in the United States — the job you save might be your own."

* * * *

Some tips from military and civilian experience.
- Don't be a clock watcher or have clock watchers around you;
- Find the smartest people around to be your assistants or aides. Do not be afraid of their taking your position;
- When seeking good executives, men or women, look for that work ethic and a good education;
- Keep an open-door policy. You never know when someone will walk in with a good idea;
- Don't work for that higher salary. Let your priority be to do the best job you can. You will be recognized and rewarded.

Let me take this opportunity to address certain readers. If you happen to be on the faculty of an institution of higher learning, I invite you to contact me through the publisher, so that I can help you get computer literacy introduced in your university. Universities that are turning out students who do not understand available computer technology and computer terminology are turning out, in terms of today's needs, illiterate students.

Toward one end of the computer world today is IBM's new Personal System-2, which they call "the broadest range of compatible personal computerizing systems ever offered." The cost is below five figures.

Toward the other end of the computer world is the Connection Machine II by Thinking Machines Corporation. It has a data-parallel system that contains 64,000 separate processors. It is like being able to read 64,000 books at one time. The cost is $1 million to $5 million .

What am I dedicated to opposing? Well, I prefer to think more in terms of what I am *for* rather than what I am *against*. But let me just quickly mention some pet peeves. I am against built-in inflation, like automatic raises. I am against tenure in the teaching profession; it dulls ambition and innovation. I am against cradle-to-grave social benefits that make it easier for a person to be on welfare than to work.

You get the message.

Let me, instead, dwell on the constructive and creative. I have work to do. It will be work towards computer literacy, toward Air Force super-development, toward assisting our youth, toward the happiness of my family. But my prime dedication is to life. Life may have some new challenges for me.

One such challenge came within the past year from a totally unexpected direction. I had to have major surgery. I was in surgery for five hours, in recovery for thirty minutes, and dismissed from the hospital in five days.

I am ready for life's challenges and am dedicated to saying yes to life. I fly life's course with enthusiasm.

John Mason Brown wrote, "No one, I am convinced, can be happy who lives only for self. The joy of living comes from immersion in something we know to be bigger, better, more enduring, and worthier than we are."

To which I say, "Amen."

GOD BLESS AMERICA